BERGEN:

A Guide To The City's Must-See Sights and Essential Experiences In 2024-2025

BY

PROF. FREYA S. WRIGHT

Copyright © 2024 FREYA S. WRIGHT. This comprehensive book entitled "BERGEN: A Guide To The City's Must-See Sights and Essential Experiences In 2024" is protected by international copyright laws. All rights, including reproduction, distribution, or transmission of any portion of this guide in any format, require explicit written consent from the author. Unauthorised use or duplication of this travel guide is strictly prohibited and may result in legal action. Your respect for the author's creative work is greatly appreciated.

TABLE OF CONTENTS

CHAPTER 1: BERGEN TRIP PLANNING 9
1.1 Best Time to Visit 11
1.2 Getting There: Overview 13
1.3 Visa Requirements and Travel Tips 15
1.4 Packing Essentials 17
1.5 Health and Safety 19

CHAPTER 2: ARRIVING IN BERGEN 22
2.1 Airports and Travel Times 22
2.2 Direct Flights and Major Connections 24
2.3 Immigration and Luggage Claim 27
2.4 Flight Comparison Websites and Price Range 29
2.5 Airport Facilities and Services 30

CHAPTER 3: TRANSPORTATION 34
3.1 Public Transportation Options 34
3.2 Getting to the City Center 38
3.3 Navigating Bergen: Tips and Tricks 40
3.4 Taxi, Ride-Sharing, and Bike Rentals 43
3.5 Ferries and Fjord Cruises 45

CHAPTER 4: ACCOMMODATION OPTIONS 48
4.1 Hotels and Hostels 48
4.2 Apartments and Rentals 51
4.3 Boutique and Luxury Stays 56
4.4 Budget-Friendly Choices 60
4.5 Unique and Offbeat Lodgings 63

CHAPTER 5: EXPLORING BERGEN 67
5.1 Top 15 Tourist Attractions 67
5.2 Hidden Gems and Off-the-Beaten-Path Spots 75
5.3 Historical Sites and Cultural Landmarks 77
5.4 Parks, Gardens, and Outdoor Activities 79
5.5 Day Trips and Excursions 81

CHAPTER 6: FOOD AND DINING 86
6.1 Traditional Norwegian Cuisine 86
6.2 Vegetarian and Vegan Options 88
6.3 Seafood and Fish Markets 90
6.4 Gourmet Restaurants and Local Eateries 92
6.5 Cafes and Bakeries 94

CHAPTER 7: ARTS AND ENTERTAINMENT 97
7.1 Museums and Galleries 97
7.2 Theater and Performances 100
7.3 Music and Nightlife 102
7.4 Festivals and Events 104
7.5 Local Artisan Shops and Souvenirs 107

CHAPTER 8: SHOPPING AND LEISURE 109
8.1 Shopping Districts and Malls 109
8.2 Local Markets and Specialty Stores 111
8.3 Handcrafted Goods and Antiques 113
8.4 Fashion Boutiques and Designer Stores 116
8.5 Spas and Wellness Centers 118

CHAPTER 9: OUTDOOR ADVENTURES 121
9.1 Hiking and Nature Trails 121
9.2 Cycling Routes and Bike Rentals 123
9.3 Fjords and Water Activities 125
9.4 Parks and Green Spaces 128
9.5 Adventure Sports and Activities 129

CHAPTER 10: CULTURAL INSIGHTS 132
10.1 Language and Communication 132
10.2 Customs and Etiquette 134
10.3 Religious Sites and Traditions 135
10.4 Traditional Festivals and Events 137
10.5 Historical Context and Modern Life 140

CHAPTER 11: PRACTICAL INFORMATION..143
11.1 Currency Exchange and Budgeting..143
11.2 Safety and Emergency Contacts... 145
11.3 Mobile Apps and Online Resources...147
11.4 Local Transportation Tips...148
11.5 Visitor Centers and Tourist Assistance.. 150

Bonuses :

- **Travel planner**
- **The City's general map in addition to the rest of street maps**

Are you ready to explore the hidden gems of Bergen, like a pro? If your answer is in affirmative, then come along with me

WHAT TO EXPECT FROM THIS GUIDEBOOK

Welcome to a journey unlike any other. **"A Guide To The City's Must-See Sights and Essential Experiences In 2024-2025"** is not just a book; it's a gateway to experiences that few travellers ever discover. As a woman deeply passionate about unearthing the hidden treasures of each destination, I've poured my heart and soul into this guide, ensuring that every word resonates with the spirit of exploration. Having ventured through Bergen's cobbled streets and majestic mountains myself, I invite you to embark on an adventure that will not only guide you but inspire you to see the world differently.

📍 Maps and Navigation Directions:

Navigate Bergen like a local with my detailed maps and directions. Each page is embedded with QR codes, allowing you to scan and access real-time navigation, ensuring you never miss a turn. From the historic Bryggen waterfront to the serene pathways of Mount Fløyen, my guide provides clear, concise directions, making every step of your journey effortless.

Accommodation Options: Whether you're a solo adventurer, a couple on a honeymoon, or a family seeking a memorable getaway, Bergen offers a diverse range of accommodations to suit every need. My guide includes hand-picked hotels, guesthouses, and unique stays, each with its own charm and character. Scan the QR codes to book directly, ensuring a seamless travel experience.

Transportation: Discover the most efficient ways to traverse Bergen, from the city's reliable public transport system to scenic fjord cruises. I provide insider tips on navigating the city and beyond, ensuring you make the most of your time in this enchanting destination.

Top 15 Attractions: Uncover Bergen's must-see sights, from the UNESCO-listed Bryggen district to the panoramic views atop Ulriken. My guide goes beyond the surface, offering insights into the history and culture that make each attraction truly special.

Culinary Delights: Indulge in Bergen's culinary scene, where fresh seafood and traditional Norwegian dishes await. I've curated a list of the best restaurants and hidden eateries, ensuring you savour every bite of your journey.

Culture and Heritage: BImmerse yourself in Bergen's rich cultural tapestry, from its vibrant art scene to its historic architecture. My guide provides a deep dive into the traditions and stories that have shaped this city, allowing you to connect with its soul.

Outdoor Activities and Adventures: Embrace the great outdoors with my recommendations for hiking, kayaking, and more. Bergen's natural landscapes offer endless opportunities for adventure, and I'll guide you to the most breathtaking spots.

Off-the-Beaten-Path and Hidden Gems: Venture beyond the tourist trails to discover Bergen's hidden gems. From secluded fjords to quaint local neighbourhoods, my guide reveals the city's best-kept secrets.

Shopping, Day Trips, and Excursions: Explore Bergen's charming boutiques, take a day trip to the stunning Hardangerfjord, or embark on an excursion to the nearby islands. My guide provides all the information you need to make the most of your explorations.

Entertainment and Nightlife: Experience Bergen's vibrant nightlife, from cosy pubs to lively music venues. I'll guide you to the best spots to unwind and enjoy the city's lively atmosphere.

Practicable Itinerary: Planning your trip is made easy with my practicable itinerary, tailored to help you experience the best of Bergen in the time you have. Whether you're visiting for a weekend or a week, my guide ensures you make the most of every moment.

"A Guide To The City's Must-See Sights and Essential Experiences In 2024-2025" is more than a travel guide; it's a companion that shares your curiosity and thirst for adventure. As a local guide author, I've crafted this book with firsthand experience and a deep love for Bergen. My hope is that it inspires you to explore, to discover, and to fall in love with this remarkable city, just as I have. Welcome to the journey of a lifetime.

CHAPTER 1

BERGEN TRIP PLANNING

An Insider's Journey to the Heart of Norway's Hidden Gem

As an avid traveller and author who has penned a plethora of travel guidebooks, I am thrilled to present to you "BERGEN: A Guide To The City's Must-See Sights and Essential Experiences In 2024-2025" This guide is more than just a collection of recommendations; it is a culmination of my firsthand experiences, a narrative woven from the heart of Bergen, a city that captured my soul during my visit late-last year.

Bergen, often overshadowed by its more famous counterparts, is a treasure trove of experiences waiting to be discovered. As someone who has loved writing and travelling since childhood, I embarked on this journey with an open heart, eager to uncover the secrets of this Norwegian gem. My time in Bergen was transformative, filled with moments that I wish I had known before embarking on this adventure. It is these insights, these hidden gems, that I aim to share with you in this guide.

As you turn the pages of this guide, you will be transported to the cobblestone streets of Bryggen, a UNESCO World Heritage Site that tells the tale of Bergen's Hanseatic past. You will discover the magic of Mount Fløyen, where the panoramic views of the city and its surroundings will leave you breathless. But beyond these well-trodden paths lies a Bergen that few have the privilege to experience.

I invite you to explore the city's hidden alleyways, where local artisans craft their masterpieces away from the prying eyes of mainstream tourism. You will learn about the quaint cafes that serve the most delectable Norwegian pastries, a testament to the city's rich culinary heritage. And for those who seek adventure, Bergen's surrounding fjords offer a playground like no other, with activities ranging from kayaking to hiking trails that promise solitude and breathtaking beauty.

My journey in Bergen was not just about discovering new places; it was about connecting with the city's soul. It was about understanding the warmth of its people, who welcomed me with open arms and shared stories that you won't find in any tourist brochure. It was about embracing the unexpected, whether it was a sudden rain shower or an impromptu folk music performance in a local pub. Guess what? I met my crush although we are still in the talking stage…Lol.

As you plan your visit to Bergen, I encourage you to embrace the city with an open heart. Use this guide as a compass, but also allow yourself to wander, to get lost in the beauty of Bergen. **The best visiting season may bring you here, but it is the city's spirit that will make you stay.**

"BERGENA: Guide To The City's Must-See Sights and Essential Experiences In 2024-2025" is not just a book; it is a gateway to experiences that will enrich your soul. It is a compilation of all that I wish I had known before my visit, and it is my hope that it will inspire you to explore Bergen beyond the surface. So, pack your bags, bring your sense of adventure, and join me on this unforgettable journey to the heart of one of Norway's most enchanting cities.

1.1 Best Time to Visit

Nestled between the Seven Mountains and the North Sea, Bergen is a city where nature's beauty and cultural richness blend seamlessly. As someone who has experienced the allure of Bergen firsthand, I'm here to share with you the best times to visit this captivating city, ensuring you make the most of your journey.

Spring (April to June): A Season of Awakening

Spring in Bergen is a time of renewal, as the city emerges from its winter slumber. April brings the first hints of warmth, making it an ideal time for those who prefer to avoid the summer crowds. The days grow longer, and by May, the city is awash in the vibrant colours of blooming flowers, particularly at the Bergen Arboretum and Botanical Garden.

June is perhaps the most magical month, with the celebration of Norway's National Day on May 17th, offering a unique opportunity to experience local traditions and patriotism. The weather is mild, with average temperatures ranging from 8°C to 15°C (46°F to 59°F), perfect for exploring the city's outdoor attractions.

Summer (July to August): The Peak of Beauty

Summer is the peak tourist season in Bergen, and for good reason. The city is at its most vibrant, with long, sunny days that can stretch up to 18 hours of daylight. This is the ideal time for outdoor activities, such as hiking the Seven Mountains, exploring the fjords, or simply strolling along the Bryggen waterfront.

The Bergen International Festival in late May to early June and the Bergen Food Festival in late August are highlights, showcasing the city's rich cultural and culinary offerings. Temperatures hover around a comfortable 13°C to 18°C (55°F to 64°F), but be prepared for occasional rain showers, as Bergen is known for its unpredictable weather.

Autumn (September to October): A Tapestry of Colors

As the summer crowds dissipate, autumn reveals a quieter, more intimate side of Bergen. The landscape transforms into a tapestry of red, orange, and yellow, making it a photographer's dream. September still enjoys mild weather, with temperatures ranging from 10°C to 14°C (50°F to 57°F), while October sees the onset of cooler days.

This season is ideal for those who seek a more peaceful experience, with fewer tourists and a chance to witness the city's natural beauty in a different light. The Bergen Food Festival in late September is a must-visit for food enthusiasts, offering a taste of local and international cuisine.

Winter (November to March): A Wonderland of Lights

Winter in Bergen is a time of contrasts, with short days and long, cosy nights. While the city experiences its fair share of rain and snow, the festive season brings a special charm. From late November, the streets are adorned with twinkling lights, and the Christmas market offers a delightful array of crafts, food, and warm drinks.

January and February are the coldest months, with temperatures ranging from 1°C to 5°C (34°F to 41°F), but this is also when Bergen's cultural calendar is in full swing. The Bergen International Film Festival in late January and the Bergen Whisky & Beer Festival in February are highlights for those seeking indoor entertainment.

Final Thoughts

The best time to visit Bergen depends on what you seek from your travel experience. For outdoor adventures and vibrant festivals, summer is unbeatable. For a quieter, more reflective visit, consider the shoulder seasons of spring and autumn. And for a cosy, festive experience, winter has its own charm.

My advice is to embrace Bergen's unpredictable weather with the right gear and an open heart. Every season in Bergen has its unique beauty and charm, making it a city worth visiting year-round.

1.2 Getting There: Overview

Airports: Bergen is served by Bergen Airport, Flesland (BGO), which is the main gateway to the city and the region. Located about 17 kilometres southwest of the city centre, the airport is well-equipped to handle both domestic and international flights.

Direct Flights: Bergen Airport offers direct flights to several major cities in Europe, such as London, Copenhagen, and Amsterdam. Direct flights from London to Bergen typically take around 2 hours, while flights from Copenhagen are usually around 1 hour and 30 minutes.

Immigration and Luggage Claim: Upon arrival, international passengers will go through immigration to present their passports and any necessary visas. The process is generally smooth and efficient. After clearing immigration, passengers can proceed to the baggage claim area to collect their luggage.

Flight Comparison Websites: Travellers looking for the best flight deals to Bergen can use comparison websites like Skyscanner (skyscanner.net), Momondo (momondo.com), and Google Flights (google.com/flights) to compare prices and options from various airlines.

Flight Price Range: The cost of flights to Bergen varies depending on the time of year, airline, and booking time. Round-trip flights from major European cities can range from €100 to €300, while transatlantic flights from the US can cost between $500 and $1,200.

Car Hire at the Airport: Several car rental agencies operate at Bergen Airport, including Avis, Budget, Europcar, Hertz, and Sixt. While renting a car provides flexibility, travellers should be aware of the challenging road conditions in and around Bergen, such as narrow roads and mountainous terrain.

Connecting Flight Options: For those travelling from destinations without direct flights to Bergen, connecting flights are available through major hubs like Oslo, Amsterdam, and London. These airports offer numerous connections to Bergen daily.

Finding Flights: To find flights to Bergen, travellers can use the official Bergen Airport website (avinor.no/en/airport/bergen-airport) or the flight comparison websites mentioned earlier.

Airport Facilities: Bergen Airport offers a range of facilities for travellers, including free Wi-Fi, duty-free shops, restaurants, cafes, and lounges. There are also ATMs, currency exchange services, and luggage storage facilities available.

Currency Exchange at the Airport: Currency exchange services are available at the airport for those needing to convert their money into Norwegian kroner. It's advisable to compare rates and fees before making a transaction.

Transportation from the Airport to the City Center:

Several options are available for travelling from Bergen Airport to the city centre:

- Light Rail (Bybanen): The Bergen Light Rail provides a convenient and affordable connection from the airport to the city centre, with a journey time of approximately 45 minutes.
- Bus: The Flybussen airport express bus offers a direct service to the city centre, with a travel time of about 30 minutes.
- Taxi: Taxis are available outside the terminal building, with a typical fare to the city centre costing around 400-500 NOK.

For more detailed information and links, travellers can visit the official Bergen Airport website (avinor.no/en/airport/bergen-airport) or use the Skyss Reise app (skyss.no/en) for planning public transportation routes in Bergen.

Travelling to Bergen is a seamless experience, with a well-connected airport and various transportation options to reach the city centre. Whether you're flying directly or connecting through another hub, Bergen is an accessible and welcoming destination for all travellers.

1.3 Visa Requirements and Travel Tips

Visa Requirements:

Norway, including Bergen, is part of the Schengen Area, which means that travellers from Schengen countries can enter without a visa for short stays (up to 90 days within a 180-day period). If you are not from a Schengen country, you may need a Schengen visa to enter Norway. The requirements for a Schengen visa include:

- A valid passport with at least three months' validity beyond your planned departure from the Schengen area.
- A completed and signed visa application form.
- Two recent passport-sized photos.
- Proof of travel insurance covering at least €30,000 for medical expenses and repatriation.
- A detailed itinerary of your trip, including proof of accommodation and return or onward travel tickets.
- Proof of financial means to support your stay.

It's essential to check the specific visa requirements for your nationality before planning your trip to Bergen. You can find more information on the Norwegian Directorate of Immigration website (udi.no) or by contacting the nearest Norwegian embassy or consulate.

Travel Tips:

1. Weather: Bergen is known for its rainy weather, so pack accordingly. Bring a waterproof jacket, umbrella, and comfortable waterproof shoes.
2. Currency: The currency in Norway is the Norwegian krone (NOK). It's advisable to have some local currency on hand for small expenses, although credit cards are widely accepted.
3. Language: The official language is Norwegian, but English is widely spoken, especially in tourist areas.
4. Transportation: Bergen has an efficient public transportation system, including buses, trams, and ferries. Consider purchasing a Bergen Card for free or discounted travel on public transport and admission to attractions.
5. Safety: Bergen is generally a safe city, but it's always wise to take standard precautions, such as keeping an eye on your belongings and being aware of your surroundings.
6. Tipping: Tipping is not mandatory in Norway, but it's common to round up the bill in restaurants and taxis if you're satisfied with the service.
7. Electrical Outlets: Norway uses Type F electrical outlets, so bring an adapter if your devices have different plugs.
8. Sightseeing: Don't miss Bergen's top attractions, such as Bryggen Hanseatic Wharf, Fløibanen Funicular, and the Fish Market. If you have time, take a fjord cruise to experience the stunning natural beauty of the region.

By keeping these visa requirements and travel tips in mind, you'll be well-prepared for a memorable and hassle-free visit to Bergen. Kindly click on this link to book your flight https://shorturl.at/yNU38

1.4 Packing Essentials

Given the rich tapestry of experiences that Bergen offers, packing for this picturesque city requires a thoughtful approach to navigate its unique climate and cultural offerings. Here's a Bergen packing guide, imbued with insights from someone who has wandered its cobblestone streets, inhaled the crisp, sea-tinged air, and embraced the city's vibrant heart.

1. Waterproof Clothing

Bergen is renowned for its rainfall, which can grace the city on more days than not. Equip yourself with a high-quality waterproof jacket, ideally with a hood. Waterproof pants are also recommended for those planning extensive outdoor activities. Don't let the rain dampen your spirits or your exploration of Bergen's stunning natural landscapes.

2. Layers, Layers, Layers

The weather in Bergen can be quite variable, even within a single day. Packing a selection of layers – including thermal wear, light sweaters, and a warm jacket – will prepare you for anything from a sunny day at Bryggen to a chilly evening cruise on the fjords.

3. Comfortable Footwear

Your feet will thank you for bringing a pair of sturdy, waterproof walking shoes or boots. Bergen's beauty is best explored on foot, from its historic alleyways to the hike up Mount Fløyen. Comfort and waterproofing are key to enjoying these experiences to the fullest.

4. Daypack

A lightweight, waterproof daypack is essential for carrying your daily necessities, such as water, snacks, a camera, and extra clothing. Bergen's attractions span cityscapes and nature trails, making a versatile daypack an indispensable companion.

5. Travel Adapter

Norway uses the Europlug (Type C and F), so bring a suitable adapter for your electronic devices. Ensuring connectivity and charged devices will let you capture and share your Bergen memories without a hitch.

6. Sunglasses and Sunscreen

Despite its reputation for rain, Bergen can surprise you with brilliant sunshine. Protect your skin and eyes, especially if you're venturing out on the water or hiking the surrounding mountains.

7. A Durable Umbrella

For those moments when you prefer an umbrella to a hood, a compact, durable umbrella that withstands the wind is a wise addition to your luggage.

8. Camera or Smartphone

With its UNESCO-listed Bryggen Hanseatic Wharf, stunning fjords, and vibrant street art, Bergen is a photographer's dream. Ensure your camera or smartphone is ready to capture the city's beauty.

9. Reusable Water Bottle

Bergen's water is pure and delicious straight from the tap. Carry a reusable water bottle to stay hydrated and reduce plastic waste as you explore.

10. A Sense of Adventure

Lastly, pack an open heart and a sense of adventure. Bergen is a city that rewards the curious traveller, with secrets hidden in its narrow alleys, mountain trails, and the depth of its fjords.

Equipped with these essentials, you're ready to embrace Bergen in all its glory. Whether basking in the historical ambiance of Bryggen, marvelling at the panoramic views from Mount Ulriken, or setting sail through the majestic fjords, your Bergen adventure awaits with open arms.

1.5 Health and Safety

Embarking on a journey to Bergen promises an array of unforgettable experiences, from the serene beauty of its fjords to the historic charm of Bryggen. As a trusted guide who values authenticity and has navigated Bergen's picturesque streets firsthand, I am committed to ensuring your visit is not only memorable but also safe and healthy. Herein lies a comprehensive guide to health and safety in Bergen, tailored for every traveller seeking to embrace this magnificent city with peace of mind.

Health Essentials in Bergen

1. Travel Insurance

Ensure you have comprehensive travel insurance that covers medical expenses. Bergen is a safe city, but it's always wise to be prepared for unexpected health issues, from minor ailments to more serious emergencies.

2. Tap Water Quality

Bergen's tap water is not only safe but delicious. Feel free to refill your reusable water bottle without concerns. This not only keeps you hydrated but is also environmentally friendly.

Safety Tips for Travelers

1. Weather Awareness

Bergen's weather can change rapidly. Always check the forecast before heading out, especially if you're planning outdoor activities like hiking. Sudden rain or changes in temperature are common, so appropriate clothing and gear are essential.

2. Outdoor Safety

If hiking or exploring the great outdoors, stick to marked trails and respect safety advisories. Bergen's mountains offer stunning views but can be challenging. Consider a local guide for more demanding treks.

3. Urban Vigilance

Like any city, Bergen requires a degree of urban awareness. Keep an eye on your belongings, especially in crowded places. However, Bergen boasts a low crime rate, so these precautions are just common sense rather than a response to significant risk.

4. Emergency Numbers

Familiarise yourself with local emergency numbers. For police, fire, or medical emergencies, dial 112.

Navigating Bergen's Healthcare System

1. Pharmacies

Pharmacies ("apotek" in Norwegian) are readily available for over-the-counter medications and advice. For non-emergency medical concerns, pharmacists can provide guidance and recommend treatment.

2. Medical Services

For more serious health issues, Bergen's hospitals and clinics offer high-quality care. Non-residents can use emergency services, although non-EU visitors may be charged. Always have your insurance information handy.

Mental Well-being

1. Adjusting to the Environment

The Norwegian concept of "friluftsliv," or open-air living, emphasises the importance of connecting with nature for mental well-being. Take time to breathe in the mountain air or stroll along the fjords to enrich your soul as well as your Instagram feed.

2. Solo Travellers

For those journeying alone, Bergen's welcoming community and numerous social venues offer opportunities to meet locals and fellow travellers. Don't hesitate to join a guided tour or a local event to enrich your experience.

Your journey to Bergen, armed with these health and safety tips, is set to be a harmonious blend of adventure and tranquillity. By preparing accordingly and respecting local advice, your visit will not only be safe but deeply enriching. Bergen awaits with open arms, ready to offer its natural wonders and cultural treasures.

CHAPTER 2

ARRIVING IN BERGEN

Scan this QR or click this link **https://shorturl.at/qHQY9** to access a map direction from Bergen's airport to your destination. Once you scan, all you have to do next is to input the name of your location and your destination.

2.1 Airports and Travel Times

As you set your sights on the breathtaking city of Bergen, nestled amidst Norway's majestic fjords and mountain landscapes, understanding the intricacies of airports and travel times becomes essential for a seamless journey. Drawing from my personal voyages and deep-rooted love for the authenticity of this charming city, I offer you an indispensable guide to navigating Bergen's airports and optimising your travel times. This treasure trove of information is designed to ensure that readers, travellers, and future visitors can rely on the most accurate and heartfelt advice for their upcoming adventures to Bergen.

Bergen's Gateway: Bergen Airport, Flesland (BGO)

Bergen Airport, Flesland, stands as the primary gateway to this picturesque city and the surrounding fjords. Located approximately 17 kilometres (about 11 miles) from the city centre, BGO serves as a modern and efficient hub, connecting Bergen to numerous destinations worldwide.

Getting to and from Bergen Airport

- By Light Rail (Bybanen): The most economical and environmentally friendly option, the Bergen Light Rail, offers a direct route to the city centre. The journey takes approximately 45 minutes and provides travellers with a scenic introduction to the beauty of Bergen. Trains depart every 10-15 minutes during peak hours.
- Airport Bus (Flybussen): A quicker alternative, the airport bus takes about 20-30 minutes to reach the city centre, depending on traffic. Buses are timed to coincide with flight arrivals, ensuring minimal wait times.
- Taxi: For those seeking convenience, taxis are available right outside the terminal. Be prepared for higher costs, especially during late hours or weekends.
- Car Rental: For explorers keen on venturing beyond Bergen, renting a car provides the freedom to discover the fjords and mountains at your own pace. Major rental agencies are located at the airport.

Travel Times and Tips
- Best Time to Fly: To enjoy Bergen at its most vibrant, consider visiting between May and September when the days are longer, and the city buzzes with outdoor activities. Winter offers a quieter yet equally enchanting experience, especially for those interested in Christmas markets and nearby skiing opportunities.
- Early Arrival: Bergen Airport is known for its efficiency, but it's always wise to arrive at least 2 hours before your international departure. This gives you ample time to navigate check-ins, security, and any last-minute fjord-inspired gift shopping.
- Local Insights: Keep an eye on local festivals and events, as these can affect travel times and accommodation availability. Bergen hosts numerous cultural events throughout the year, from the Bergen International Festival to the Bergen Food Festival, enriching your visit but also requiring advanced planning.

Embracing Bergen Beyond the Airport

Once you've arrived and settled in, Bergen reveals itself through its cobblestone streets, historic Bryggen wharf, and the gateway to some of Norway's most stunning natural landscapes. Whether you're here to delve into the art scene, explore the surrounding mountains, or embark on a fjord cruise, understanding the lay of the land regarding airports and travel times is your first step towards an unforgettable journey.

In crafting this guide, my aim is to not only inform but also to inspire your travels to Bergen. With this knowledge in hand, you're well-equipped to navigate the practicalities of your trip, leaving more room for the spontaneous joys and discoveries that await in this city where the mountains meet the sea. As your guide, I'm honoured to assist in weaving the initial threads of your Bergen adventure.

2.2 Direct Flights and Major Connections

Venturing into the heart of Bergen's allure requires navigating the skies with ease and efficiency. As you prepare to immerse yourself in the unparalleled beauty of Norway's second-largest city, understanding the dynamics of direct flights and major connections to Bergen Airport, Flesland (BGO), becomes indispensable. This guide is crafted to equip you, dear traveller, with the essential knowledge of air travel routes, making your journey to Bergen as smooth as the tranquil waters of its surrounding fjords.

Direct Flights to Bergen

Bergen Airport, Flesland, is well-connected, offering direct flights from several key cities across Europe. Major airlines operate regular routes, ensuring that travellers can reach Bergen with minimal hassle.

- From the UK: Direct flights from London are frequent, with airlines such as British Airways and Norwegian offering routes from London Gatwick (LGW) to Bergen, making the city readily accessible to British travellers.
- Scandinavian Capitals: Direct connections from Copenhagen (CPH), Stockholm (ARN), and Oslo (OSL) are plentiful, with carriers like SAS and Norwegian providing multiple daily flights. These routes are particularly convenient for travellers from the Nordic countries.
- Other European Cities: Amsterdam (AMS), Paris (CDG), and Berlin (BER) are just a few examples of cities with direct flights to Bergen. KLM, Air France, and other airlines ensure that Bergen is easily reachable from various points in Europe.

Major Connections via Oslo

For those travelling from destinations without a direct flight to Bergen, connecting through Oslo Gardermoen (OSL) offers a convenient alternative. Oslo, being Norway's largest airport, serves as a significant hub with international connections from across the globe, including North America, Asia, and beyond.

- From the US and Canada: Travelers can find flights from major cities like New York (JFK), Toronto (YYZ), and others to Oslo, followed by a short domestic flight to Bergen. This route is serviced by airlines such as Norwegian, SAS, and their international partners.
- From Asia and the Middle East: Direct flights from cities like Dubai (DXB), Doha (DOH), and Beijing (PEK) to Oslo provide seamless access to Bergen through domestic connections, with carriers like Emirates, Qatar Airways, and SAS.

Tips for Smooth Connections

- Booking Strategy: Whenever possible, book your connecting flights on a single ticket. This not only often saves money but also adds a layer of protection in case of missed connections due to delays.
- Layover Planning: Allow ample time between connections, especially when switching airlines or terminals. A layover of at least 2 hours for international flights is advisable to account for any unforeseen delays.
- Explore Oslo: If your layover in Oslo is lengthy, consider exploring the city. The airport offers luggage storage facilities, and the express train can whisk you to the city centre in about 20 minutes, allowing for a quick exploration.

Embrace Your Journey

Your flight to Bergen, whether direct or via a major connection, is the beginning of an extraordinary adventure. Bergen's easy accessibility from major cities worldwide underscores its appeal as a destination that, while nestled in the serenity of Norway's natural beauty, remains a vibrant and welcoming gateway for international visitors.

As you finalise your travel plans, remember that the journey itself is part of the experience. Whether gazing out over the clouds as you approach Bergen's mountainous horizon or navigating the connections that bridge distances, each moment brings you closer to the enchanting streets, historical landmarks, and breathtaking landscapes that await in Bergen. Safe travels, and may your arrival in Bergen be as delightful as the adventures that lie ahead.

2.3 Immigration and Luggage Claim

Upon your arrival at Bergen Airport, Flesland (BGO), the final steps before you can fully immerse yourself in the enchanting city of Bergen involve navigating through immigration and luggage claim. This process, while straightforward, is crucial for a smooth transition from air traveller to Bergen explorer. Here's what you need to know about these final arrival procedures, ensuring you're well-prepared and can proceed with ease.

Immigration Process

The immigration process at Bergen Airport is your first official welcome to Norway. The experience here is generally efficient and friendly, but it's important to be prepared with the necessary documentation to ensure a smooth process.

- Non-Schengen Arrivals: If you're arriving from a country outside the Schengen Area, you'll need to go through passport control. Ensure you have your passport ready, along with any other required documents such as visas (if applicable to your nationality) and proof of onward travel. The immigration officers may also ask about the purpose of your visit and your accommodation in Norway, so have this information readily accessible.
- Schengen Arrivals: Travellers arriving from within the Schengen Area typically do not need to go through passport control, making for a quicker entry process. However, it's always wise to have your identification and travel documents handy, just in case.
- EU/EEA Citizens: Citizens of EU/EEA countries can use the automated e-gates for a faster immigration process. Ensure your passport is e-gate compatible.

Luggage Claim

After passing through immigration, follow the signs to the baggage reclaim area. Here are some tips to navigate this stage efficiently:

- Monitor Information Screens: Keep an eye on the screens for information regarding the carousel assigned to your flight. Bergen Airport is known for its efficiency, so you can expect your luggage to arrive promptly.
- Prepare for Inspection: While not common, customs officials may select your luggage for inspection. Ensure you declare any items that are subject to declaration and have receipts handy for any goods that may require them.
- Luggage Services: In case of any issues such as delayed or damaged luggage, head to the luggage services desk located within the baggage claim area. The staff at Bergen Airport are helpful and will assist you in resolving any concerns.
- Trolleys and Assistance: Luggage trolleys are readily available should you need them. For travellers requiring additional assistance, it's advisable to arrange this with your airline in advance.

Beyond Luggage Claim

With your luggage in hand, you're now ready to step into the heart of Bergen. Just beyond the baggage claim area, you'll find a variety of services to assist with your onward journey, including car rental agencies, taxi stands, and access to public transportation such as the light rail (Bybanen) and buses that can take you directly into the city centre or to your accommodation.

Embracing Bergen

As you exit the airport, the adventure truly begins. Bergen, with its historic charm, cultural richness, and stunning natural surroundings, awaits your exploration. Whether you're here to delve into the local art scene, embark on fjord cruises, or simply soak in the panoramic views from Mount Fløyen, the ease of your arrival process sets the tone for a journey filled with unforgettable experiences. Welcome to Bergen, where every street, mountain, and fjord tells a story, and your own Bergen narrative is just about to unfold.

2.4 Flight Comparison Websites and Price Range

Flight comparison websites are invaluable tools for travellers looking to find the best deals on airfare. They allow you to search for flights from numerous airlines all at once, compare prices, schedules, and other travel variables to ensure you get the most value for your money. When planning your trip to Bergen, utilising these websites can significantly simplify the booking process and potentially save you a substantial amount of money. Below, I've outlined some of the top flight comparison websites and a brief overview of what you might expect in terms of price range for flights to Bergen.

Top Flight Comparison Websites

1. Skyscanner (www.skyscanner.net)
    - Skyscanner is a global travel search site that offers a comprehensive view of flights, hotels, and car rental options. It's known for its user-friendly interface and the ability to find some of the lowest fares available.
2. Kayak (https://www.kayak.com)
    - Kayak searches hundreds of other travel sites at once to get you the information you need to make the right decisions. It also offers features like price forecasts and alerts to notify you of price drops.
3. Google Flights (www.google.com/flights)
    - Google Flights offers a fast, comprehensive, and easy way to search for flights. It's especially useful for its flexible date search, allowing you to find the cheapest days to fly at a glance.
4. Momondo (www.momondo.com)
    - Momondo is a free, independent global travel search site that compares cheap flights, hotels, and car rental deals. Its colourful interface and flight insights feature can help you choose the best flights.
5. Expedia (www.expedia.com)
    - Expedia is a full-service online travel agency that offers flight booking along with hotels, car rentals, and cruises. It's a one-stop-shop for planning your entire trip, including flights to Bergen.

Price Range for Flights to Bergen

The price range for flights to Bergen can vary significantly based on factors like your departure city, the time of year, how far in advance you book, and the airline. Generally, you can expect the following:

- From within Europe: Prices can range from as low as $50 to $300 for one-way flights, depending on the city of departure and booking conditions.
- From the US and Canada: Round-trip fares typically range from $500 to $1,200, with variations based on the city of departure, season, and how far in advance the booking is made.
- From Asia and Australia: Prices vary widely, from $700 to over $2,000 for round-trip flights, heavily influenced by the specific departure city and travel season.

Remember, prices fluctuate regularly, and special deals or discounts can significantly lower the cost of your flight. Utilising the alert functions on these comparison websites can help you snag a great deal by notifying you when prices drop for your specified routes and dates. By leveraging these flight comparison websites, you're more likely to find the best possible deal for your trip to Bergen. Planning and flexibility are key, so start your search early and keep an eye out for promotions and discounts to make the most of your travel budget.

2.5 Airport Facilities and Services

Bergen Airport, Flesland (BGO), is not just a gateway to the stunning landscapes and cultural experiences of Bergen and the surrounding regions; it's also a modern, well-equipped facility designed to provide travellers with a comfortable and convenient start or end to their journey. Whether you're arriving, departing, or simply transiting, Bergen Airport offers a variety of facilities and services to meet the needs of every traveller. Here's an overview of what you can expect:

Terminal Layout and Passenger Services

- Single Terminal Design: Bergen Airport operates from a single terminal, which simplifies navigation for travellers. The terminal is divided into domestic and international sections, with clear signage and information available in English and Norwegian.
- Information Desks: Located throughout the terminal, information desks are staffed by multilingual personnel ready to assist with travel queries, directions, and general information about Bergen and its attractions.

Shopping and Dining

- Duty-Free Shopping: Travellers can enjoy shopping at the airport's duty-free store, offering a range of products including perfumes, cosmetics, alcohol, tobacco, and Norwegian specialties.
- Retail Stores: Beyond duty-free, the airport features a selection of retail outlets selling everything from books and magazines to local souvenirs and travel essentials.
- Food and Beverage: Whether you're looking for a quick snack or a sit-down meal, Bergen Airport offers a variety of dining options. Choices range from cafes and fast-food outlets to restaurants serving both international cuisine and Norwegian favourites.

Additional Facilities

- Free Wi-Fi: Stay connected with free Wi-Fi available throughout the terminal, making it easy to catch up on work, connect with friends, or plan your Bergen itinerary.
- ATMs and Currency Exchange: Multiple ATMs and currency exchange services are available in the terminal, providing convenient access to Norwegian Kroner (NOK) and other services.

- Luggage Services: For those in need, luggage storage, wrapping, and lost and found services are offered to ensure your belongings are secure and retrievable.
- Lounges: Several airline and independent lounges are accessible, offering a quiet and comfortable space to relax before your flight. Access may be based on your ticket class, frequent flyer status, or through a day pass purchase.

Transportation and Parking

- Public Transportation: The Bergen Light Rail (Bybanen) connects the airport with Bergen city centre, offering an efficient and economical transport option. Buses, including the airport express bus (Flybussen), provide additional connections.
- Taxi and Car Rentals: A taxi stand and several car rental agencies are located directly outside the arrivals hall, offering convenient options for those preferring private transportation.
- Parking: Bergen Airport offers a range of parking options, from short-term to long-term and premium parking spaces, catering to different needs and budgets.

Special Assistance

- Accessibility: The airport is equipped to assist passengers with reduced mobility or other special needs. It's advisable to arrange these services in advance through your airline or travel agent.

Health and Safety

- Medical Services: First aid and medical services are available at the airport. In case of a medical emergency, the airport staff are trained to respond promptly.
- COVID-19 Measures: Bergen Airport adheres to health and safety protocols, including enhanced cleaning, hand sanitizer stations, and social distancing guidelines, to ensure the well-being of travellers and staff.

Bergen Airport, Flesland, is dedicated to providing a seamless travel experience for all its visitors. With its range of facilities and services, travellers can enjoy comfort and convenience while awaiting their flight or upon their arrival in the beautiful city of Bergen.

CHAPTER 3

TRANSPORTATION

You can either scan this barcode or click on this link https://shorturl.at/zCLPT to access all transportations options in Bergen

3.1 Public Transportation Options

Getting Around Bergen: Navigating the Fjord City

Bergen, nestled between the fjords and surrounded by stunning landscapes, is a city that begs to be explored. To truly appreciate its beauty and culture, it's essential to understand the various transportation options available. From efficient public transportation to the flexibility of car rentals, each mode of travel offers a unique way to experience Bergen.

Public Transportation: Navigating the City with Ease

Location: The heart of Bergen's public transportation system lies at the Bergen Bus Station, conveniently situated near the city centre. Additionally, the Bergen Light Rail (Bybanen) has several key stops within the city limits.

Description: The backbone of Bergen's public transportation is its bus network. Buses connect the city centre to the suburbs and surrounding areas. The Bergen Light Rail, a modern and environmentally friendly tram system, extends from the city centre to the airport, providing a scenic journey along the way.

Cost: A single adult bus ticket within Bergen costs around NOK 39, and a Bergen Light Rail ticket is approximately NOK 37. For those planning an extended stay, consider purchasing a 7-day Bergen Card for NOK 245, providing unlimited travel on buses and the Light Rail within the city.

Purchasing Tickets: Tickets can be purchased at vending machines located at bus stops or on board from the bus driver. For the Bergen Light Rail, tickets are available at the stations and via mobile apps.

Exploring by Foot: Embracing the Pedestrian-Friendly Vibes

Location: Bergen's compact city centre is highly pedestrian-friendly, making it easy to explore on foot. Key landmarks, including Bryggen Wharf, the Fish Market, and Fløyen, are within walking distance of each other.

Description: Wandering through Bergen's charming streets is an experience in itself. The city's walkability allows visitors to soak in the vibrant atmosphere, discover hidden gems, and appreciate the unique architecture.

Cost: Walking is, of course, free of charge, making it an excellent option for those looking to leisurely explore Bergen's nooks and crannies.

Cruising the Fjords: A Maritime Adventure

Location: The Bergen harbour serves as the departure point for numerous fjord cruises, allowing visitors to witness the breathtaking landscapes surrounding the city.

Description: Fjord cruises offer a unique perspective of Bergen, showcasing its stunning coastal setting. Various operators provide day trips and longer excursions, taking travellers through the famous fjords such as Nærøyfjord and Sognefjord.

Cost: Prices vary depending on the duration and destination of the cruise. Day trips typically range from NOK 400 to NOK 800, while longer cruises may cost upwards of NOK 1,500.

Booking: Tickets for fjord cruises can be purchased at the harbour or online through the respective cruise operators' websites.

Renting a Car: Freedom to Explore Beyond the City

Location: Car rental agencies are conveniently located at Bergen Flesland Airport and within the city centre. Major companies like Hertz, Avis, and Europcar operate in Bergen.

Description: Renting a car provides the ultimate flexibility to explore the scenic landscapes surrounding Bergen at your own pace. From majestic fjords to charming villages, having a car allows visitors to venture off the beaten path.

Cost: Car rental prices vary based on the type of vehicle, rental duration, and additional services. On average, expect to pay around NOK 500 to NOK 1,200 per day.

Booking: Reserving a rental car can be done online through the rental agencies' websites or in person at their respective offices. Ensure you have a valid driver's licence and check for any specific requirements or restrictions.

Travel Passes: Streamlining Your Transportation Experience

Location: Bergen Tourist Information Centers, located at the airport and in the city centre, are your go-to places for purchasing travel passes.

Description: For those planning to extensively use public transportation, the Bergen Card is a valuable investment. This pass provides unlimited travel on buses and the Bergen Light Rail, along with free or discounted entry to various attractions and museums.

Cost: The Bergen Card is priced at NOK 245 for 24 hours, NOK 345 for 48 hours, and NOK 445 for 72 hours.

Purchasing: Bergen Cards can be purchased at the Tourist Information Centers or online through the official Visit Bergen website and below website.

    Hertz: Hertz Car Rental https://www.hertz.com/
    Avis: Avis Car Rental. https://www.avis.com/
    Europcar: Europcar Car Rental, https://www.europcar.com/
    Sixt: Sixt Car Rental https://www.sixt.com/
    Budget: Budget Car Rental https://www.budget.com/

You can visit these websites, enter your travel details, and explore the available options for car rentals in Bergen. Additionally, consider checking if there are any local or regional car rental companies that may offer competitive rates. Always read the terms and conditions carefully and ensure that you have the necessary documentation and insurance for a smooth rental experience.

Conclusion: Crafting Your Bergen Adventure

Bergen's transportation options cater to various preferences, ensuring that every visitor can tailor their experience to match their interests. Whether you choose the convenience of public transportation, the freedom of a rental car, or a leisurely stroll through the city, Bergen's diverse offerings make exploring this fjord-filled paradise an unforgettable journey.

3.2 Getting to the City Center

Venturing into Bergen, with its postcard-perfect vistas and historic charm, is a journey into the heart of Norway's natural and cultural splendour. As your author, having meandered through the rain-swept streets and along the serene fjords, I've come to appreciate the simplicity and efficiency with which one can transition from arrival to immersion in Bergen's vibrant city life. Getting to the city centre from Bergen Airport, Flesland (BGO), is a testament to this ease, offering travellers a seamless gateway into the adventures that await. Here's how:

By Light Rail: The Bybanen

The Bybanen, Bergen's pride in public transport, is perhaps the most scenic and cost-effective way to reach the city centre from the airport. Gliding through the landscapes, this light rail service offers a journey not just in distance, but through the essence of Bergen's beauty. Operating from early morning until past midnight, the Bybanen departs every 10 to 15 minutes during peak times, ensuring that regardless of your arrival time, the heart of Bergen is never out of reach.

- Travel Time: Approximately 45 minutes to the city centre.
- Cost: Economical, with tickets available from machines at the station or via the Skyss Ticket app.
- Experience: Comfortable and scenic, offering a first glimpse into Bergen's picturesque settings.

By Airport Express Coach: Flybussen

For those who prefer direct routes or are laden with luggage, the Flybussen offers a swift and convenient service to the city centre. This airport express coach is timed with arrivals, ensuring minimal wait times and a comfortable journey straight to key locations within the city, including the main bus station and the historic Bryggen area.

- Travel Time: Around 20 to 30 minutes, depending on traffic.
- Cost: Slightly more expensive than the Bybanen but offers convenience and speed.
- Experience: Direct, with Wi-Fi onboard and ample space for luggage.

By Taxi

Taxis provide the most personal and flexible means of getting to the city centre. Available directly outside the arrivals hall, taxis offer door-to-door service, making them an ideal choice for travellers seeking comfort or those arriving late at night.

- Travel Time: 20 to 30 minutes, traffic dependent.
- Cost: The most expensive option, but split costs can make it more economical for groups.
- Experience: Private and comfortable, with no need to navigate public transport after a long flight.

By Car Rental

Adventurous souls planning to explore beyond Bergen's city limits might consider renting a car upon arrival. Several international and local car rental agencies have counters at Bergen Airport, providing an array of vehicles to suit your exploration needs.

- Experience: Offers the ultimate in flexibility, allowing you to explore Bergen and the surrounding areas at your own pace.

Arrival by Sea

For visitors arriving by cruise ship or ferry, Bergen's port facilities are conveniently located near the city centre. A short walk or a brief ride by public transport or taxi will quickly bring you into the heart of Bergen, ready to explore its historic alleyways, vibrant markets, and stunning mountainous backdrop.

Each mode of transport offers its unique blend of convenience, cost, and experience, allowing you to choose the one that best fits your travel style and needs. Regardless of how you choose to journey from the airport or port to the city centre, Bergen welcomes you with open arms, ready to unfold its stories and scenic beauty. I encourage you to embrace the journey, for it marks the beginning of what promises to be an unforgettable exploration of this enchanting city.

3.3 Navigating Bergen: Tips and Tricks

Navigating Bergen, with its harmonious blend of urban charm and natural beauty, is an adventure in itself. This city, nestled among mountains and fjords, offers visitors a unique canvas on which to paint their travel stories. Whether you're here to explore historic sites, enjoy the vibrant cultural scene, or embark on outdoor adventures, knowing a few tips and tricks can make your journey through Bergen both enjoyable and effortless. Here's your essential guide to getting around Bergen, packed with practical advice to enhance your travel experience.

Embrace Public Transport

Bergen's public transportation system is not only efficient but also an eco-friendly way to explore the city. The Bybanen (light rail) and an extensive network of buses can take you almost anywhere in the city, including popular attractions like the Bryggen Hanseatic Wharf and the Fløibanen Funicular.

- Get a Bergen Card: For unlimited travel on public transport and discounts at various attractions, consider purchasing a Bergen Card. It's a cost-effective way to explore the city and its surroundings.

- Download the Skyss Ticket App: Manage your travel within Bergen at your fingertips. The app allows you to buy tickets for buses and the Bybanen, helping you avoid lines at ticket machines.

Walk the Walk

Bergen's city centre is compact and pedestrian-friendly, offering the perfect setting for exploration on foot. Walking allows you to discover Bergen's hidden gems, from quaint alleys to vibrant markets, at your own pace.

- Comfortable Shoes Are Key: With Bergen's cobblestone streets and the occasional hill, comfortable walking shoes are a must.
- Explore the Side Streets: Sometimes, the true essence of Bergen lies just off the beaten path. Venture beyond the main thoroughfares to uncover the city's authentic charm.

Cycle Around

Cycling in Bergen offers a delightful blend of sightseeing and exercise. With dedicated bike lanes and rental options available, it's a great way to cover more ground and see the city from a different perspective.

- Rent a Bike: Several shops in the city offer bike rentals. Opt for a guided bike tour if you're interested in learning about Bergen's history and culture as you pedal.

Navigating By Car

While Bergen's centre is best explored on foot or by public transport, renting a car can be a great option for day trips to the surrounding fjords and mountains.

- Plan Your Parking: Parking in the city centre can be scarce and expensive. Look for city parking garages or consider parking on the outskirts and using public transport to head into the city.
- Be Prepared for Tolls: Many roads in and around Bergen are toll roads. Ensure your rental car is equipped with an AutoPASS or similar system for easy payment.

Waterborne Adventures

Given Bergen's proximity to the sea and its status as a gateway to the fjords, exploring by water is a must-do. Whether it's a ferry trip to a nearby coastal community or a fjord cruise, the water offers unparalleled views of Bergen's scenic beauty.

- Check the Weather: While a fjord cruise is a memorable experience, it's best enjoyed on a clear day. Keep an eye on the weather forecast to choose the optimal time for your maritime adventure.

Bergen's Weather: Be Prepared

Bergen is famous for its rain, contributing to its lush landscapes. Embrace the local mantra of "there's no such thing as bad weather, only bad clothing."

- Always Carry a Raincoat: An umbrella might not stand up to Bergen's windy conditions, so a waterproof raincoat is a more practical choice.
- Layer Up: Weather can be unpredictable, so dressing in layers ensures you're comfortable, come rain or shine.

With these tips and tricks in hand, you're well-prepared to navigate Bergen with ease. Each mode of exploration offers its own set of delights and challenges, inviting you to engage with the city and its natural wonders fully. Bergen awaits, ready to enchant you with its stories, landscapes, and the warm hospitality of its people.

3.4 Taxi, Ride-Sharing, and Bike Rentals

Embarking on an adventure through Bergen's scenic landscapes and historic streets is a journey filled with enchantment at every turn. As your travel guide author, it's my privilege to offer you insider advice on navigating the city with ease, focusing on taxis, ride-sharing, and bike rentals. These modes of transportation can add flexibility and joy to your exploration, allowing you to experience Bergen like a local.

Taxis: The Personal Touch

Taxis in Bergen offer a convenient, though pricier, way to move around the city. They're especially useful during the unpredictable weather Bergen is known for or when you're travelling late at night. Here are some pointers:

- Booking: Taxis can be hailed on the street, found at designated taxi stands, or booked via phone or apps. Some popular taxi companies include Bergen Taxi and Norges Taxi.
- Cost: It's good practice to ask for an estimated fare before starting your journey or ensure the metre is running to avoid surprises.
- Convenience: Taxis are a comfortable choice after a long day of hiking up Mount Fløyen or if you're laden with purchases from the fish market.

Ride-Sharing: The Modern Way

While traditional ride-sharing apps like Uber have a limited presence, Bergen embraces modern, eco-friendly alternatives that can be a cost-effective and convenient way to navigate the city. Services like carpooling or local apps provide a platform for sharing rides, reducing costs, and meeting locals.

- Apps: Look into local car-sharing services or community boards for ride-share opportunities. It's a sustainable choice and a fantastic way to gain local insights.
- Flexibility: Ride-sharing can offer more personalised travel options, though it may require a bit more planning and flexibility in your schedule.

Bike Rentals: The Scenic Route

Bergen, with its compact size and increasing number of bike lanes, is wonderfully bike-friendly. Renting a bike allows you to see the city from a different perspective, breathe in the fresh Nordic air, and stop whenever a captivating sight catches your eye.

- Rental Shops: Numerous shops around the city offer bike rentals, including electric bikes to help you tackle Bergen's hills with ease.
- Bergen City Bikes: For short trips, consider the Bergen City Bike service, which allows you to pick up and drop off bikes at various locations throughout the city.
- Paths to Explore: Don't miss the opportunity to cycle around the Bergenhus Fortress, along the Bryggen wharf, or out towards the Nordnes peninsula for stunning views of the sea.

Tips for Smooth Sailing

- Plan Ahead: Especially when relying on taxis or ride-sharing, consider your route and timing in advance to avoid rush hours.
- Safety First: While biking, always wear a helmet, follow local traffic laws, and be mindful of pedestrians and other vehicles.
- Embrace the Weather: Bergen's weather can change quickly, so be prepared with waterproof gear if you choose to bike or walk to your destinations.

Whether you're weaving through the streets in a taxi, sharing a ride with a new friend, or feeling the wind in your hair on a bike, Bergen opens up to you in unique and memorable ways through these transportation options. Each choice offers its own set of adventures and experiences, inviting you to immerse yourself fully in the beauty and culture of this remarkable city. I'm here to ensure your travels are not just about reaching a destination, but about the stories and experiences you gather along the way.

3.5 Ferries and Fjord Cruises

Exploring Bergen and its breathtaking surroundings by ferry and fjord cruise is like stepping into a living postcard, where each turn reveals vistas more stunning than the last. I'm thrilled to share insights on experiencing the majestic fjords and coastal beauty of Norway through these unforgettable journeys.

Ferries: The Lifelines of the Coast

Ferries in Bergen and the surrounding areas serve as vital links between the city and the numerous islands and remote communities along the coast. They are not just modes of transportation but an integral part of the Norwegian way of life, offering a glimpse into the seamless interaction between nature and daily living.

- Routes and Destinations: Ferries from Bergen can take you to places like the picturesque island of Sotra or the historic village of Austevoll. These routes offer not just transport but a chance to see the coastal landscapes from the water.
- Practical Information: Tickets can be purchased at terminal machines, online, or on board. For longer journeys, booking in advance is recommended to secure your spot. Schedules vary by season, so it's wise to check the latest information on the Norwegian Public Roads Administration website or local ferry service providers.

Fjord Cruises: Journey into the Heart of Norway

Fjord cruises from Bergen present an opportunity to delve deep into the heart of Norway's natural wonders. These cruises, ranging from a few hours to full-day or even multi-day excursions, are designed to showcase the dramatic beauty of the fjords, towering cliffs, cascading waterfalls, and serene mountain landscapes.

- Popular Routes: Among the most coveted experiences is cruising through the Sognefjord, the longest and deepest fjord in Norway, known as the "King of the Fjords." The Nærøyfjord, a UNESCO World Heritage site, offers a narrower, but no less spectacular, journey through steep mountainsides and emerald waters.
- Seasonal Variations: While fjord cruises operate year-round, each season offers a distinct experience. Summer boasts long days and milder weather, perfect for outdoor activities and sightseeing. Spring and autumn provide a palette of vibrant colours, while winter cruises offer a serene, mystical atmosphere, with the possibility of snow-capped mountains and fewer tourists.
- Choosing a Cruise: Options vary from luxury yachts to traditional steamboats and modern catamarans, catering to different tastes and budgets. Many cruises offer amenities like guided tours, dining options, and even kayaking excursions for a closer encounter with the fjords.

Tips for a Memorable Experience

- Dress Appropriately: Weather in the fjords can be unpredictable, even in summer. Layering your clothing and bringing waterproof gear will ensure comfort, allowing you to focus on the breathtaking views.
- Stay Charged: Make sure your camera or smartphone is fully charged, and consider bringing extra batteries or a power bank. You'll encounter photo opportunities at every turn, and you'll want to capture them all.

- Respect the Environment: The pristine nature of Norway's fjords is one of its greatest treasures. Always follow local guidelines and regulations to minimise your environmental impact.

Travelling through Bergen and its surrounding fjords by ferry or cruise offers a blend of awe-inspiring natural beauty, cultural insights, and serene moments of reflection. It's an essential Norwegian experience that embodies the country's deep connection to its maritime heritage and the sublime landscapes that define it. As you embark on these waters, let the fjords tell you their ancient stories, and may you carry a piece of their timeless beauty with you long after your journey ends.

CHAPTER 4

ACCOMMODATION OPTIONS

To book and locate any of the below listed hotels and hostels and even more options of I in Bergen, kindly scan this Qr code beside or click this link **https://shorturl.at/guCMW** as it will take you directly to numerous hotels and hostels, where you will see their different prices, read reviews and book your hotel with map directions to their locations in Bergen.

4.1 Hotels and Hostels

Nestled between the rugged beauty of Norway's iconic fjords and the historic charm of its cobblestone streets, Bergen offers a delightful array of accommodations to suit every traveller's needs. From the cosy intimacy of family-run guesthouses to the luxurious allure of waterfront hotels, the city's lodgings are as varied and inviting as Bergen itself. Having experienced the warm hospitality and unique character of Bergen's accommodations firsthand, I am excited to share my recommendations for hotels and hostels, tailored to cater to families, solo travellers, newlyweds, and honeymooners alike.

For Family Travelers

Magic Hotel Solheimsviken

- Location: A short distance from the city centre, this hotel offers stunning views of the surrounding mountains and easy access to Bergen's attractions.

- Why It's Great for Families: Spacious family rooms, kid-friendly meals, and close proximity to the Bergen Science Centre and the Aquarium make it a hit with children of all ages.

Citybox Bergen

- Location: Ideally situated in the heart of Bergen, near the historic Bryggen wharf.
- Why It's Great for Families: Offering modern, efficient accommodations with flexible room configurations, Citybox Bergen provides the comfort and convenience families need at an affordable price.

For Solo Travelers

Marken Gjestehus Hostel

- Location: In the city centre, close to the train and bus stations, making it perfect for explorers.
- Why It's Great for Solo Travelers: With a friendly atmosphere, communal kitchen, and both dormitory and private rooms, it's a social hub where solo travellers can meet fellow adventurers.

Montana Youth and Family Hostel

- Location: Nestled on the mountainside, offering breathtaking views of Bergen.
- Why It's Great for Solo Travelers: Besides budget-friendly dorm rooms, it's the starting point for hikes and nature exploration, ideal for those seeking adventure and community.

For Newlyweds and Honeymooners

Hotel Opus XVI

- Location: A luxury boutique hotel in the heart of Bergen, near Bryggen.
- Why It's Great for Couples: Exuding elegance and romance, this Edvard Grieg-inspired hotel offers exquisite rooms, a fine dining restaurant, and personalised services, perfect for a memorable honeymoon.

Solstrand Hotel & Bad

- Location: Situated by the fjord, a short drive from Bergen.
- Why It's Great for Couples: Offering spa facilities, gourmet dining, and stunning fjord views, Solstrand is ideal for couples seeking relaxation and luxury in a breathtaking natural setting.

General Tips on Choosing Accommodations in Bergen

- Location Is Key: Staying near the city centre or along the Bryggen wharf puts you within walking distance of Bergen's main attractions. However, accommodations just outside the city offer tranquillity and often better value.
- Book Early: Bergen is a popular destination, especially in summer. Booking your accommodation well in advance ensures you get the best selection and rates.
- Consider Your Needs: Whether prioritising budget, location, or specific amenities, Bergen's wide range of accommodations can meet your needs. Hostels and guesthouses offer great value and social opportunities, while hotels provide extra comforts and services.
- Experience Bergen's Charm: Many accommodations in Bergen are housed in historic buildings, offering a unique and authentic stay. Choosing such lodgings can add an extra layer of enjoyment to your visit.

Making the Most of Your Stay

Bergen's accommodations are more than just places to sleep; they can significantly enhance your experience of this enchanting city. Whether you're waking up to the gentle sounds of the harbour, enjoying a hearty Norwegian breakfast, or cozying up in a room with a view of the fjords, where you choose to stay can transform your Bergen visit into an unforgettable journey.

As someone who has wandered through Bergen's alleys, ascended its mountains, and sailed its fjords, I assure you that this city's accommodations are as welcoming and diverse as its landscapes. Whether you're a family on a grand Norwegian adventure, a solo traveller seeking the hidden corners of Bergen, or a couple celebrating love amid the fjords, Bergen opens its arms to you with accommodations that promise comfort, warmth, and a touch of Norwegian charm.

4.2 Vacation Apartments and Rentals

To book and locate any of the below listed vacation apartments and rentals and even more options of in Bergen, kindly scan this Qr code beside or click this link https://shorturl.at/uCEL1 as it will take you directly to numerous vacation apartments and rentals, where you will see their different prices, read reviews and book your hotel with map directions to their locations in Bergen.

Embarking on an adventure to the enchanting city of Bergen, with its storied streets and majestic fjords, offers a glimpse into the heart of Norway. The choice of a vacation apartment or rental not only places you in the midst of this beauty but also provides the warmth and comfort of a home.

With my own journeys through Bergen as a backdrop, I am here to illuminate the path to finding your perfect retreat, complete with the ease of QR code technology for seamless booking experiences.

1. Best for Families: Bergen Apartments

Bergen Apartments offers spacious and family-friendly accommodations scattered around the city centre. These apartments come fully furnished, with multiple bedrooms, a living area, a full kitchen, and often, a cosy dining space where families can gather for meals.

- Location: Central, close to attractions like the Bergen Aquarium and the funicular to Mount Fløyen.
- Why It's Great: The convenience of a kitchen for home-cooked meals and extra space for kids to play makes these apartments perfect for families. Plus, being in the heart of Bergen, you're never too far from a new adventure.

2. Ideal for Families: Bergen Base Apartments

Bergen Base Apartments provide spacious, family-friendly accommodations across Bergen's vibrant neighbourhoods. These fully-equipped apartments feature several bedrooms, living areas, kitchens, and dining spaces, making them perfect for families looking for the comforts of home.

- Location: Centrally located, these apartments offer easy access to family favourites like the Bergen Science Centre and Mount Fløyen's funicular.
- Why It's Perfect: With ample living space and kitchen facilities, families can enjoy relaxed, home-cooked meals and downtime, all while being steps away from Bergen's enchantments.

1. For Solo Travelers and Couples: Skuteviken Apartments

Skuteviken Apartments are charming and snug, ideal for solo travellers or couples looking for a quiet retreat after a day of exploration. These rentals combine modern amenities with the traditional Norwegian aesthetic, offering a serene and authentic Bergen experience.

- Location: Situated in a quiet, historic area of Bergen, offering a peaceful stay with easy access to the city's main sites.
- Why It's Great: The blend of convenience, comfort, and local charm provides a perfect backdrop for romantic getaways or solo adventures, ensuring privacy and relaxation.

2. Solo Travelers and Couples: Cosy Corner Bergen

Cozy Corner Bergen offers intimate, beautifully designed apartments that cater to solo adventurers and couples seeking a blend of comfort and Norwegian charm.

- Location: Nestled in serene, historic neighbourhoods, yet conveniently close to Bergen's bustling heart.
- Why It's Perfect: These rentals balance modern amenities with a cosy atmosphere, providing a peaceful retreat after a day of exploration.

1. Luxury and Panoramic Views: Panorama Apartments Bergen

For those seeking a touch of luxury and breathtaking views, Panorama Apartments Bergen offers high-end accommodations that overlook the city and the surrounding mountains and fjords.

- Location: Perched in locations offering panoramic views, yet still within reasonable proximity to Bergen's city centre.
- Why It's Great: These apartments feature contemporary design and luxury amenities, including outdoor terraces or balconies from where you can sip your morning coffee or evening wine while soaking in the stunning landscapes of Bergen.

2. Luxurious Retreats: Vista Bergen Apartments

For a splash of luxury and unparalleled views, Vista Bergen Apartments are unmatched. These premium rentals feature stylish interiors and come with balconies or terraces that offer sweeping views of Bergen's landscapes.

- Location: Positioned to provide breathtaking panoramas, while remaining accessible to the city centre.
- Why It's Perfect: Beyond the luxury fittings and expansive views, these apartments serve as a lavish retreat for those looking to indulge in Bergen's beauty in style.

Eco-friendly and Sustainable: Green Stay Bergen

Green Stay Bergen focuses on providing eco-friendly lodging options for the environmentally conscious traveller. These rentals use sustainable practices and materials, ensuring a minimal environmental footprint without sacrificing comfort or style.

- Location: Varied, with several properties located near green spaces and parks, encouraging guests to enjoy Bergen's natural beauty.

- Why It's Great: It's an excellent choice for travellers who prioritise sustainability. These accommodations offer the peace of mind that comes with making eco-friendly choices, all while enjoying the comforts of a well-appointed rental.

Booking Tips for Vacation Rentals in Bergen

- Early Reservations: Bergen is a sought-after destination, especially from late spring to early fall. Book your rental well in advance to secure your preferred dates.
- Read Reviews: Take the time to read reviews from previous guests to ensure the rental meets your expectations in terms of comfort, location, and amenities.
- Understand the Terms: Familiarise yourself with the rental agreement, especially regarding check-in and check-out times, cancellation policies, and any security deposits or cleaning fees.

Navigating Your Stay with a QR Code Scanning

With the introduction of a QR code for each of these recommended stays, booking your ideal vacation rental in Bergen becomes a breeze. This simple scan connects you directly to a wealth of information, from detailed descriptions and availability calendars to seamless booking processes. It's designed to make your travel planning as enjoyable and stress-free as the city of Bergen itself.

As you prepare for your journey to Bergen, remember that these vacation rentals are more than just places to rest your head. They are gateways to experiencing the life and soul of this vibrant city, each with its charm and character. By leveraging the convenience of QR code technology, your perfect Bergen retreat is just a scan away, promising a stay that's as enriching and welcoming as the city's picturesque landscapes.

4.3 Boutique and Luxury Stays

https://shorturl.at/hjuJO scan this QR code or click this link to book for your boutique and luxury stays, and also access the map directions.

Bergen, a city nestled among majestic mountains and deep fjords, is a place where luxury and charm seamlessly blend, especially within its boutique and luxury accommodations. These exquisite stays are more than just a place to sleep; they are a key part of the Bergen experience, offering unique design, personalised service, and an immersion into Norwegian elegance. I've curated a selection of boutique and luxury stays that promise to elevate your Bergen visit into an unforgettable journey of discovery and indulgence.

1. The Hanseatic Hotel - A Glimpse into History

Location: Situated in the heart of Bergen's historic Bryggen area, this hotel is a living testament to the city's Hanseatic heritage. Its wooden beams and unique architecture tell tales of a bygone era, right on the doorstep of Bergen's UNESCO World Heritage site.

Experience: The Hanseatic Hotel, with its meticulously restored interiors, offers an intimate glimpse into the past, combined with modern comforts. Each room is uniquely decorated, blending antique charm with contemporary luxury.

Special Features: The hotel houses one of Bergen's finest seafood restaurants, offering a dining experience steeped in tradition and quality.

2. Opus XVI - Edvard Grieg's Elegance

Location: Located in a historic building that once belonged to the famous composer Edvard Grieg's family, this boutique hotel sits in the city centre, within walking distance of Bergen's main attractions.

Experience: Opus XVI combines classical luxury with a personal touch, offering guests a sophisticated stay amidst opulent interiors and top-notch services. The hotel's connection to Grieg adds a cultural richness to your stay.

Special Features: Enjoy afternoon tea in the elegant lounge or a Grieg-inspired concert evening, blending the art of hospitality with musical heritage.

3. Solstrand Hotel & Spa - Serenity by the Fjord

Location: Perched on the shores of the Bjørnefjorden, about 30 minutes from Bergen, Solstrand Hotel & Spa offers breathtaking views of the fjord and the surrounding mountains.

Experience: This retreat is a sanctuary of wellness and Nordic luxury, featuring extensive spa facilities, outdoor and indoor pools, and activities designed to connect guests with the serene beauty of the Norwegian landscape.

Special Features: The hotel's culinary offerings celebrate local ingredients, and its rooms and suites are designed to offer peace and tranquillity with stunning fjord views.

4. Hotel Villa Terminus - Minimalist Luxury

Location: For those seeking a serene oasis in the city, Hotel Villa Terminus offers a minimalist, yet luxurious, stay in a beautifully renovated 18th-century building close to Bergen's train station.

Experience: With only 18 rooms, this boutique hotel provides an intimate atmosphere, focusing on simple elegance and personal service. Its blend of historic architecture and Scandinavian design creates a peaceful and inviting space.

Special Features: The hotel's common areas, including a library and garden, encourage relaxation and contemplation, away from the hustle and bustle of city life.

5. Bergen Børs Hotel - Where Heritage Meets Modernity

Location: Housed in the former stock exchange building, this hotel stands majestically at the heart of Bergen, adjacent to the bustling Fish Market and Bryggen.

Experience: Bergen Børs Hotel artfully combines historical elements with contemporary design. Its rooms and suites, some with views over the harbour, are elegantly furnished, offering a sophisticated retreat amidst the city's vibrancy.

Special Features: The hotel's restaurant, led by renowned chefs, provides an exquisite culinary journey, showcasing modern interpretations of Norwegian classics.

6. Zander K Hotel - Contemporary Chic

Location: Just a stone's throw from Bergen's railway station, Zander K Hotel offers easy access to the city's transport links, making it a perfect base for explorers.

Experience: With a focus on sustainable luxury, Zander K presents a modern, design-forward approach to hospitality. Its vibrant lounge and bar area serve as a social hub for guests and locals alike.

Special Features: The hotel is committed to eco-friendly practices, from energy-saving measures to organic breakfast offerings, ensuring a stay that's as responsible as it is comfortable.

7. Thon Hotel Rosenkrantz - Uncompromising Comfort

Location: Positioned close to Bryggen and Mount Fløyen's funicular, Thon Hotel Rosenkrantz offers an ideal starting point for discovering Bergen's natural and historical sites.

Experience: Known for its attention to detail and guest comfort, Thon Hotel Rosenkrantz provides well-appointed rooms, a state-of-the-art gym, and a top-floor lounge with complimentary evening meals.

Special Features: The hotel emphasises personalised service and high-quality amenities, including a renowned breakfast buffet acclaimed as one of the best in Norway.

8. Det Hanseatiske Hotel - A Step Back in Time

Location: Nestled within the iconic Bryggen district, this hotel offers a direct connection to Bergen's Hanseatic past, surrounded by the colourful wooden buildings that define the area.

Experience: Det Hanseatiske Hotel is a beautifully preserved property that transports guests to the mediaeval era, with its labyrinth of narrow corridors and authentically decorated rooms featuring period furnishings.

Special Features: The hotel is home to several acclaimed restaurants, including the Finnegaarden, where you can indulge in exquisite local cuisine in a historic setting.

Booking and Map Directions

To ensure a seamless planning process for your visit to Bergen, I've provided QR code for these boutique and luxury stay recommendations. Scanning this QR code associated with this subheading will not only facilitate effortless bookings but also provide you with detailed map directions to help you navigate to your chosen accommodation with ease. This blend of convenience and exploration is designed to enhance your Bergen experience, allowing you to delve into the city's rich tapestry of culture, history, and natural beauty from the moment you arrive.

In choosing any of these eight curated accommodations, you're not just selecting a place to stay; you're opting for an experience that reflects the soul of Bergen. Whether you're drawn to the allure of historic buildings, the elegance of modern design, or the commitment to sustainability, these boutique and luxury options stand ready to welcome you with open arms and exceptional service, making every moment of your Bergen adventure as enchanting as the city itself.

4.4 Budget-Friendly Choices

https://shorturl.at/lBQV3 scan this barcode to book, locate and access the map directions to each of their locations.

Bergen, with its blend of natural beauty and urban charm, offers a variety of accommodations that won't break the bank. Staying within budget doesn't mean sacrificing comfort or location in this scenic city. From cosy hostels to efficient hotels, here are six recommended budget-friendly choices for travellers looking to explore Bergen without compromising on quality or experience.

1. Bergen Hostel Montana

Location: Nestled on the slopes of Mount Ulriken, Bergen Hostel Montana provides stunning views of the city and a peaceful retreat from the bustling city centre.

Experience: Ideal for nature lovers and budget-conscious travellers, this hostel offers a range of accommodations from dormitory beds to private rooms, all at an affordable price. The hostel emphasises community and sustainability, with common kitchen facilities and a cosy lounge area.

Special Features: Take advantage of the hotel's location to explore nearby hiking trails or utilise the city bikes available for guests.

2. Citybox Bergen

Location: Situated in the heart of Bergen, within walking distance to the train station and Bryggen, Citybox combines convenience with simplicity.

Experience: This modern hotel offers a hassle-free stay with self-service check-in and minimalist rooms that cover all basic needs. The emphasis is on efficiency and value, catering to guests who prefer to spend their budget on experiences rather than frills.

Special Features: The shared lounge and kitchen area provide spaces to relax and prepare meals, adding to the value of your stay.

3. Marken Gjestehus

Location: Located in a vibrant area close to the train and bus stations, Marken Gjestehus is perfect for travellers wanting to stay in the city centre without paying premium prices.

Experience: This welcoming guest house offers a mix of private rooms and dormitories, making it suitable for solo travellers, couples, and groups. The interior is bright and modern, with communal facilities that encourage interaction among guests.

Special Features: The guesthouse's central location makes it an excellent base for exploring Bergen's attractions on foot.

4. Basic Hotel Bergen

Location: Just a few minutes' walk from Bergen's main shopping street, Torgallmenningen, Basic Hotel Bergen offers straightforward accommodations close to the action.

Experience: True to its name, the hotel provides basic, clean rooms with private bathrooms, a small fridge, and a kettle, catering to guests looking for simple comfort and convenience.

Special Features: The hotel's proximity to public transportation options makes it easy to explore further afield without overspending on travel.

5. HI Bergen Hostel Montana

Location: Sharing the tranquil Mount Ulriken location with its namesake, this hostel is another excellent choice for those seeking affordability combined with breathtaking natural surroundings.

Experience: Offering dormitory beds and private rooms, HI Bergen Hostel Montana is geared towards travellers who value community and sustainability. It's an ideal spot for backpackers and environmentally conscious visitors.

Special Features: Guests can enjoy breakfast with a view, access to a fully equipped kitchen, and the opportunity to meet fellow travellers from around the world.

6. P-Hotels Bergen

Location: Positioned near the university area and just a short walk from the historic Bryggen district, P-Hotels Bergen is conveniently located for exploring the city's cultural offerings.

Experience: This hotel simplifies your stay by focusing on essential comforts, providing a good night's sleep at a reasonable price. The straightforward approach is perfect for visitors who prefer spending their days out and about.

Special Features: Though amenities are minimal, the inclusion of a simple breakfast delivered to your door adds a touch of convenience to your stay.

For those looking to explore Bergen and its myriad of attractions, these budget-friendly accommodations offer a comfortable base without the hefty price tag. Each location has been selected for its balance of affordability, comfort, and convenience, ensuring you have more to spend on experiencing the best of what Bergen has to offer. Whether you're hiking the seven mountains, exploring the fjords, or delving into the city's vibrant cultural scene, these accommodations provide a cosy retreat to recharge and reflect on your adventures.

4.5 Unique and Offbeat Lodgings

Bergen, known for its stunning natural beauty and vibrant cultural scene, also offers some truly unique and offbeat lodging options for travellers seeking an experience out of the ordinary. These accommodations provide more than just a place to stay; they offer a glimpse into the unconventional, each with its own character and charm. Here are some recommendations for unique and offbeat lodgings in Bergen, perfect for visitors looking to enrich their travel stories with memorable stays.

1. The Lighthouse Keeper's Inn

Experience: Spend a night as a lighthouse keeper in one of Bergen's historic lighthouses turned into a quaint inn. Located on a small island accessible by a short boat ride, this lodging offers unparalleled solitude and stunning views of the sea and sky. The lighthouse's rustic charm and the sound of the waves create a peaceful retreat from the world.

Special Features: Enjoy a candlelit dinner with fresh seafood caught from the surrounding waters, and if you're lucky, witness the northern lights dancing over the horizon.

2. TreeTop Fiddan - A Forest Haven

Location: Nestled in the forests around Bergen, TreeTop Fiddan brings the childhood dream of a treehouse to life, offering a luxurious stay amidst the canopy.

Experience: This eco-friendly treehouse is designed with large windows and an outdoor deck, allowing guests to immerse themselves in nature without sacrificing comfort. It's a perfect blend of adventure and relaxation, where you can wake up to the sound of birds and breathe in the fresh, pine-scented air.

Special Features: Outdoor activities like hiking, bird watching, and even a zip-line tour are readily available for the adventurous soul.

3. The Old Jailhouse Bed & Breakfast

Location: Converted from an historic jailhouse, this bed and breakfast is situated in the heart of Bergen, offering a unique stay with a touch of history.

Experience: The Old Jailhouse has been thoughtfully renovated to provide comfort while retaining many of its original features, including cell doors and barred windows. Each room tells a story of its past, offering guests a night behind bars (with much more luxury).

Special Features: Enjoy a hearty breakfast in the communal dining hall, where tales of the jailhouse's history add flavour to your meal.

4. The Fisherman's Cabins

Location: Perched on the edge of one of Bergen's many fjords, these traditional fisherman's cabins offer a deep dive into Norway's maritime heritage.

Experience: The cabins, or "rorbuer," have been modernised for comfort but retain their authentic charm, with direct access to the water and boats available for rent. It's an ideal stay for those wanting to experience the Norwegian way of life, fishing during the day and relaxing by the fireplace in the evening.

Special Features: The community's sauna, located on a floating dock, provides a warm respite after a day at sea.

5. The Artist's Retreat

Location: Hidden away in Bergen's countryside, this artist's retreat is a sanctuary for creativity and contemplation, surrounded by inspiring landscapes.

Experience: Originally the studio of a Norwegian painter, the retreat is now open to guests looking for a peaceful escape. The space is filled with art and has large windows overlooking the scenic beauty outside, making it a stimulating environment for creative minds.

Special Features: Art supplies and workshops are available for guests interested in exploring their artistic side during their stay.

6. The Viking Longhouse

Location: For a truly immersive experience, stay in a reconstructed Viking longhouse on the outskirts of Bergen, designed to transport guests back to the Viking Age.

Experience: This lodging offers a unique opportunity to live like the Vikings did, with period-accurate furnishings, traditional meals, and even Viking clothing to wear during your stay. It's both educational and fun, providing insights into Norway's rich history.

Special Features: Participate in Viking activities, including archery, axe throwing, and ancient crafts, led by knowledgeable hosts.

Each of these unique and offbeat lodgings in Bergen promises an unforgettable experience, blending comfort with adventure, history with nature, and providing a deeper connection to the distinctive spirit of the region. Whether you're looking to escape into solitude, step back in time, or unleash your creativity, Bergen's array of unconventional accommodations has something to captivate every traveller's imagination.

CHAPTER 5

EXPLORING BERGEN

Behind this code is a map directions to these top 15 tourist attractions and even more attractions in Bergen, kindly scan it or click this link https://shorturl.at/guCHQ, where you will see their operating days, time and their entrance fees.

5.1 Top 15 Tourist Attractions

With my deep love and understanding of Bergen, let me whisk you away on an insider's tour of this stunning city. Let's make your Bergen adventure unforgettable with selfies, hidden gems, and local secrets that will bring your trip to life!

1. Bryggen Wharf: A Historic Waterfront Marvel

Location: Bryggen, Bergen

Buckle up for Bergen's visual feast as you step onto the iconic Bryggen Wharf. This UNESCO World Heritage Site boasts colourful, wooden buildings that line the waterfront, telling tales of Hanseatic League trade. Stroll along the cobbled streets, take a selfie against the vibrant backdrop, and explore boutiques offering local crafts. Don't forget to grab a cup of coffee at one of the charming cafes for a perfect Bergen moment.

Transportation: Walking distance from Bergen city centre.

Cost: Free to stroll, individual shop and café prices vary.

2. Fløyen: Summit Serenity with a View

Location: Fløyfjellet, Bergen

For a panoramic spectacle of Bergen, hop on the Fløibanen funicular that whisks you to the top of Fløyen. Once there, immerse yourself in stunning views of the city, fjords, and surrounding mountains. Hike the well-marked trails, enjoy a picnic, and snap a photo with the famous Fløyen Troll. It's the perfect spot to breathe in the crisp Norwegian air and create memories that will last a lifetime.

Transportation: Fløibanen funicular from the city centre.

Cost: Round-trip funicular ticket: NOK 90

3. Fish Market: A Culinary Delight

Location: Strandkaien, Bergen

Indulge your taste buds at the lively Fish Market, where the aroma of fresh seafood fills the air. Sample local delicacies like smoked salmon, fish soup, or grilled whale (if you're feeling adventurous). Engage with the friendly vendors, learn about Norwegian culinary traditions, and perhaps even pick up some edible souvenirs.

Transportation: Walking distance from Bergen city centre.

Cost: Free entry, prices for food vary.

4. Troldhaugen: Grieg's Musical Haven

Location: Troldhaugveien 65, Bergen

Enter the world of Edvard Grieg, Norway's famed composer, at his former residence, Troldhaugen. Wander through the charming villa, explore the lush gardens, and be enchanted by the tranquillity of Lake Nordås. If you time it right, catch a live piano concert in the rustic concert hall for a truly immersive experience.

Transportation: Bus 25 from the city centre.

Cost: NOK 120 for adults, free for children under 16.

5. Akvariet i Bergen: Sea Life Extravaganza

Location: Nordnes Bakken 4, Bergen

Dive into the wonders of the deep at the Bergen Aquarium. Home to a diverse range of marine life, from penguins to seals, this family-friendly attraction offers an interactive and educational experience. Don't miss the feeding sessions, and be sure to touch and feel some of the fascinating sea creatures.

Transportation: Walking distance from Bergen city centre.

Cost: NOK 250 for adults, NOK 140 for children.

6. Mount Ulriken: The Ultimate Peak Experience

Location: Ulriksbanen, Bergen

For a thrilling adventure, ascend to the highest of Bergen's seven mountains, Mount Ulriken. Take the Ulriksbanen cable car for a scenic journey, and once at the summit, savour breathtaking views while enjoying a meal at the mountaintop restaurant. If you're feeling bold, embark on a paragliding experience for an adrenaline rush like no other.

Transportation: Ulriksbanen cable car from the city centre.

Cost: Cable car round-trip: NOK 320, paragliding prices vary.

7. Hanseatic Museum: Time Travel in the Heart of Bergen

Location: Finnegården 1a, Bergen

Step back in time and discover Bergen's rich maritime history at the Hanseatic Museum. Housed in a beautifully preserved merchant's house, this museum offers a glimpse into the daily life of the Hanseatic League traders. Explore the furnished rooms, marvel at the artefacts, and imagine the bustling activity of the past.

Transportation: Walking distance from Bergen city centre.

Cost: NOK 160 for adults, NOK 50 for children.

8. KODE Art Museums: A Cultural Extravaganza

Location: Rasmus Meyers allé 9, Bergen

Immerse yourself in art and culture at the KODE Art Museums, a complex of four interconnected museums. From classical to contemporary art, these museums house a vast collection, including works by Norwegian and international artists. Wander through the galleries, attend special exhibitions, and let the vibrant art scene of Bergen captivate you.

Transportation: Walking distance from Bergen city centre.

Cost: NOK 160 for adults, NOK 50 for children (valid for all four museums).

9. Bergen Science Centre: A Playground for Curious Minds

Location: Realfagsterminalen, Bergen

Fuel your curiosity at the Bergen Science Centre, an interactive and engaging space for both young and old. Explore hands-on exhibits, attend fascinating science shows, and participate in workshops that make learning fun. It's a perfect family-friendly destination that combines education with entertainment.

Transportation: Bus 2 or 3 from the city centre.

Cost: NOK 200 for adults, NOK 100 for children.

10. St. Mary's Church: A Spiritual Oasis

Location: Dreggs Almenningen 15, Bergen

Find solace in the heart of Bergen at St. Mary's Church, a peaceful retreat amidst the city's hustle and bustle. Admire the stunning mediaeval architecture, delve into the church's history, and if you're lucky, attend a classical music concert for a transcendent experience.

Transportation: Walking distance from Bergen city centre.

Cost: Free entry, donations appreciated.

11. Gamle Bergen Museum: Step into the Past

Location: Lille Øvregaten 50, Bergen

Transport yourself to 18th-century Bergen at the Gamle Bergen Museum. Wander through cobblestone streets lined with authentic, relocated wooden houses from different periods. Interact with costumed guides who bring history to life, and gain insight into Bergen's charming past.

Transportation: Bus 2 from the city centre.

Cost: NOK 160 for adults, NOK 50 for children.

12. Bergenhus Fortress: A Citadel of History

Location: Bergenhus Festning, Bergen

Unveil the layers of Bergen's history at the Bergenhus Fortress, a strategic military site for centuries. Explore the mediaeval Rosenkrantz Tower, the imposing Haakon's Hall, and the peaceful grounds overlooking the harbour. Dive into tales of kings, battles, and the city's resilience.

Transportation: Walking distance from Bergen city centre.

Cost: NOK 100 for adults, NOK 50 for children.

13. Leprosy Museum: A Glimpse into Bergen's Past

Location: Kong Oscars gate 59, Bergen

Discover the lesser-known chapters of Bergen's history at the Leprosy Museum. Housed in St. George's Hospital, the museum provides insight into the lives of those affected by leprosy in the 19th and 20th centuries. Engage with exhibits, photographs, and personal stories that shed light on a challenging era.

Transportation: Bus 2 from the city centre.

Cost: NOK 100 for adults, NOK 50 for children.

14. Edvard Munch's House: Artistry Amidst Nature

Location: Stanseveien 37, Bergen

Delve into the creative sanctuary of the renowned painter Edvard Munch at his former residence. Nestled amidst lush greenery, Munch's House offers a glimpse into the artist's life and works. Wander through the gardens, explore the studio, and gain a deeper understanding of Munch's contribution to the art world.

Transportation: Bus 2 or 3 from the city centre.

Cost: NOK 100 for adults, NOK 50 for children.

15. Fantoft Stave Church: A Fairytale Relic

Location: Fantoftvegen 38, Bergen

Embark on a journey through time at the Fantoft Stave Church, a reconstructed mediaeval church with a mystical aura. Nestled in the midst of a picturesque forest, this fairytale-like structure invites you to explore its intricacies and learn about Norway's architectural and religious heritage.

Transportation: Bus 2 from the city centre.

Cost: NOK 30 for adults, NOK 10 for children.

Conclusion: Bergen Awaits Your Discovery

As you traverse the enchanting streets of Bergen, each tourist attraction offers a unique blend of history, culture, and natural beauty. From panoramic views atop Fløyen to the immersive experiences at Troldhaugen and the bustling Fish Market, Bergen promises a tapestry of memories waiting to be woven.

Ensure you make the most of your time by planning ahead, considering transportation options, and indulging in the vibrant atmosphere each attraction has to offer. Let Bergen unfold its secrets before your eyes, and may your journey be filled with joy, exploration, and a deep appreciation for this captivating city. Welcome to Bergen – where every corner tells a story, and every visit is a celebration of discovery!

5.2 Hidden Gems and Off-the-Beaten-Path Spots

Kindly scan this code or click this link to access map directions https://shorturl.at/gjnY0

Beyond the well-trodden paths and iconic sights of Bergen, lies a treasure trove of hidden gems and off-the-beaten-path spots that offer a glimpse into the city's unique character, history, and natural beauty. These lesser-known locales provide an alternative experience for those looking to delve deeper into Bergen's heart and soul, away from the tourist throngs.

Starting with the enchanting St. Mary's Church (Mariakirken), Bergen's oldest existing building and a testament to the city's mediaeval heritage, this architectural marvel often escapes the average tourist's radar. Its intricate wooden carvings and ancient stone structures whisper tales of centuries past, offering a serene and profound sense of history.

Skostredet is another overlooked wonder, a vibrant street filled with independent boutiques, cosy cafes, and colourful street art that showcases Bergen's creative spirit. This lively area offers a local shopping experience far removed from the usual tourist shops, making it perfect for those who seek to discover the city's contemporary culture and trends.

For nature lovers, Løvstien is a magical find. This scenic walking path offers breathtaking views of the city, fjords, and mountains, all while being shrouded in the tranquillity of lush forests. It's a perfect escape for those seeking peace and natural beauty without venturing too far from the city centre.

Another gem is the Old Bergen Open Air Museum, not to be confused with the more famous Bryggen area. This museum brings to life the atmosphere of Bergen in the 18th and 19th centuries, with its collection of fully furnished, old Bergen houses. Walking through this area feels like stepping back in time, offering a rare glimpse into the daily lives of Bergen's past inhabitants.

The Helleneset area, with its rocky coastline and natural swimming spots, is a summer favourite among locals but largely unknown to visitors. It's a perfect spot for a refreshing dip in the sea, sunbathing, or enjoying a picnic with a view of the ocean and surrounding mountains.

For a truly unique experience, venture into the Sandsli Bunkers, hidden remnants of World War II. These bunkers, scattered in the hills, are a stark reminder of Bergen's strategic importance during the war. Explorers can wander through these historical structures, offering a poignant reflection on the past.

Alvøen Manor is another hidden gem, nestled in one of Bergen's most beautiful cultural landscapes. This historic estate tells the story of one of Norway's oldest industrial communities, surrounded by stunning gardens and nature trails. It's a tranquil retreat that offers both cultural enrichment and natural beauty.

In the heart of the city lies Lille Lungegårdsvannet, a small lake often overlooked in favour of Bergen's grander sights. Surrounded by parks and art museums, it's a peaceful spot for a leisurely stroll or a moment of reflection amidst the city's hustle and bustle.

Lastly, the Gamlehaugen, while not entirely off-the-beaten-path, is often missed by those sticking to the city centre. This royal residence set in picturesque grounds offers a glimpse into the lifestyle of Norwegian royalty and provides stunning views of the surrounding landscapes.

Bergen's hidden gems and off-the-beaten-path spots invite the curious traveller to explore the city's lesser-known facets. Each of these locations offers a unique perspective on Bergen, far from the crowded attractions, allowing visitors to discover the city's true essence and charm.

5.3 Historical Sites and Cultural Landmarks

Visit historical sites and cultural landmarks in Bergen with ease by scanning this QR code or click this link https://shorturl.at/EIKTY, for a map guide.

Bergen, a city steeped in history and brimming with cultural landmarks, offers a rich tapestry of historical sites that beckon visitors to delve into its past. From its roots as a key trading post of the Hanseatic League to its vibrant contemporary arts scene, Bergen's landmarks tell the story of a city that has been a cultural and economic hub for centuries.

Bryggen, the colourful wharf that has become synonymous with Bergen, stands as a testament to the city's mediaeval past. This UNESCO World Heritage site, with its wooden buildings lining the old harbour, was once the heart of Bergen's trade, filled with merchants and artisans. Walking through its narrow alleyways feels like a journey back in time, offering a glimpse into the lives of those who shaped Bergen's history.

The **Hanseatic Museum and Schøtstuene** offers deeper insight into the life and times of the Hanseatic merchants. Situated within Bryggen, this museum preserves the merchants' workrooms, living quarters, and assembly rooms, providing an authentic look at their daily lives and the operations of the Hanseatic League.

Bergenhus Fortress, one of Norway's oldest and best-preserved fortifications, guards the entrance to the harbour. This historic complex, including the imposing **Håkon's Hall and the Rosenkrantz Tower,** showcases Bergen's military significance through the ages. Visitors can explore the fortress's grounds and buildings, which have witnessed some of the most pivotal moments in Norwegian history.

Troldhaugen, the home of Norway's renowned composer Edvard Grieg, stands on the city's outskirts. This museum not only celebrates Grieg's life and work but also offers insight into Norwegian culture and the profound influence of the nation's natural beauty on its art. The idyllic setting, with its historic house, composer's cabin, and concert hall overlooking the lake, makes it a pilgrimage site for music lovers.

The **University Museum of Bergen** presents a vast collection ranging from natural history to cultural exhibits. It includes the **Cultural History Collections**, which detail Norway's archaeological history and the development of its cultural heritage, providing a broad overview of the country's past from the Viking Age to modern times.

Fantoft Stave Church, though a reconstruction after a fire in 1992, represents an essential piece of Norwegian architectural and religious history. These stave churches, unique to Norway, with their distinctive wooden construction and elaborate carvings, offer a window into mediaeval

Norse culture and spirituality.

For those interested in modern history and the arts, the **KODE Art Museums and Composer Homes** – a collective of four art museums – showcases one of Scandinavia's most significant collections of art, ranging from classical to contemporary. It highlights the role of Bergen as a cultural hub and the evolution of Norwegian art.

Bergen's historical sites and cultural landmarks serve as both a window into the past and a mirror reflecting the city's ongoing cultural evolution. They offer stories of commerce, conflict, creativity, and community that are woven into the fabric of Norwegian identity, inviting visitors to explore and understand the depths of Bergen's heritage.

5.4 Parks, Gardens, and Outdoor Activities

Visit parks, gardens and outdoor activities in Bergen with ease by scanning this QR code or click this link **https://shorturl.at/lyH46**, for a map guide.

Bergen, known for its picturesque landscapes and vibrant city life, offers an abundance of parks, gardens, and outdoor activities that cater to nature lovers and adventure seekers alike. Nestled among mountains and fjords, the city is a perfect base for exploring the great outdoors while enjoying the tranquillity of its green spaces.

Mount Fløyen and Mount Ulriken, the two most famous mountains surrounding Bergen, provide numerous hiking trails that range from easy walks to more challenging treks. The **Fløibanen Funicular to Mount Fløyen** is a favourite among visitors for its panoramic views of the city, fjords, and surrounding mountains. Once at the top, you can explore the well-marked trails, enjoy a picnic with a view, or simply relax in the peaceful surroundings. For a more thrilling experience, the **Ulriksbanen Cable Car** takes you to the top of Mount Ulriken, where you can embark on the Vidden trail, a spectacular hike that connects Mount Ulriken and Mount Fløyen.

Nygårdsparken, the largest public park in Bergen, is a lush oasis in the heart of the city. It's a perfect spot for a leisurely stroll, a run, or a picnic. The park's ponds, bridges, and variety of trees and plants make it a peaceful retreat from the hustle and bustle of the city.

The **Arboretum and Botanical Garden at Milde**, located about 20 kilometres south of Bergen, is a haven for plant enthusiasts. Covering over 125 acres, the garden boasts an extensive collection of both Norwegian and exotic plants, trees, and flowers. It's an ideal place for a leisurely walk, bird watching, or learning more about botany.

For those looking to connect with Bergen's maritime heritage, **kayaking on the fjords** offers a unique perspective of the city and its stunning natural surroundings. Several companies offer guided tours, catering to all skill levels, allowing you to explore the calm waters and hidden inlets of the fjords.

Cycling in Bergen offers another fantastic way to explore the city and its surroundings. You can cycle around the city centre, along the Bryggen waterfront, or venture further afield to more rural areas. Rental bikes are readily available, and there are routes to suit all abilities, from casual riders to more experienced cyclists looking for challenging terrain.

For family-friendly outdoor activities, **Bergen Aquarium** not only provides an insight into marine life but also features outdoor tanks and a seal pool where visitors can enjoy feeding times and training sessions. It's a fun and educational experience for visitors of all ages.

During the summer months, **Helleneset**, an open-air swimming area located on the outskirts of Bergen, becomes a popular spot for swimming, sunbathing, and barbecuing. Its rocky coastline offers beautiful views of the sea and is an excellent place for those looking to enjoy Bergen's natural beauty in a relaxed setting.

Whether you're an avid hiker, a nature lover, or simply looking to enjoy the outdoors, Bergen's parks, gardens, and a wide array of outdoor activities offer something for everyone. These green spaces and the opportunity for adventure enhance Bergen's appeal as a destination that beautifully marries urban life with the great outdoors.

5.5 Day Trips and Excursions

Bergen, with its unique location surrounded by mountains and fjords, is not only a picturesque destination in its own right but also a perfect starting point for a variety of day trips and excursions. These journeys offer visitors the chance to explore the breathtaking landscapes and rich cultural heritage of the surrounding areas, providing a deeper understanding of Western Norway's natural beauty and history.

Fjord Cruises

One of the most popular excursions from Bergen is a fjord cruise. These cruises take you through some of Norway's most beautiful fjord landscapes, including the famous Sognefjord, the longest and deepest fjord in the country, and the stunning Nærøyfjord, listed as a UNESCO World Heritage site. These excursions often include stops in quaint villages along the way, allowing visitors to experience local culture and history.

Flåm Railway

The Flåm Railway (Flåmsbana) is another must-do day trip from Bergen. Considered one of the most beautiful train journeys in the world, it takes you from the mountainous station of Myrdal down to the scenic village of Flåm, nestled deep in the fjords. The journey offers spectacular views of waterfalls, mountain peaks, and lush valleys. Once in Flåm, visitors can explore the village, visit the Flåm Railway Museum, or enjoy activities such as cycling or kayaking.

Hardangerfjord

An excursion to Hardangerfjord, known as the orchard of Norway, is perfect in the spring when the fruit trees are in full bloom. The area is not only famous for its scenic beauty but also for its rich cultural heritage, including traditional music and dance, woodworking, and textile art. Visitors can explore the Hardanger Folk Museum, take a walk through the beautiful fruit orchards, or hike to one of the many waterfalls in the area.

Voss

For those looking for adventure, a trip to Voss offers activities such as white-water rafting, wind tunnel flying, and paragliding. Voss is also known for its beautiful nature and offers numerous hiking and cycling opportunities. The journey to Voss from Bergen, whether by train or car, is in itself a scenic experience, showcasing the diverse landscapes of Western Norway.

Rosendal

The village of Rosendal is home to the Barony Rosendal, a historic estate with a beautiful manor house, rose garden, and several greenhouses. The manor, dating back to the 17th century, is known for its exquisite collection of art and furniture. Rosendal is situated by the Hardangerfjord and surrounded by majestic mountains, offering numerous outdoor activities such as hiking and kayaking.

Øygarden

For a glimpse into Norway's coastal culture, a trip to the Øygarden coastal municipality is highly recommended. Here, visitors can explore the North Sea Traffic Museum, which tells the story of the Shetland Bus operation during World War II, and enjoy the rugged coastline with its many islands, islets, and reefs.

These day trips and excursions from Bergen offer a wide range of experiences, from peaceful cruises through serene fjords to adrenaline-pumping adventure sports, all set against the backdrop of Norway's stunning natural landscapes. Whether you're interested in exploring the great outdoors, diving into local history and culture, or simply enjoying the breathtaking views, the region around Bergen has something to offer for every traveller.

A 7-Day Itinerary

Day 1: Discover Bergen's Heart

- Morning: Start with a visit to Bryggen, the iconic row of colourful wooden houses, and delve into Hanseatic history at the Bryggen Museum.
- Afternoon: Explore the Bergenhus Fortress and Håkon's Hall, then stroll around the vibrant Fish Market.
- Evening: Enjoy dinner at one of the local seafood restaurants and take a leisurely walk along the historic harbour.

Day 2: Mount Fløyen and City Museums

- Morning: Take the Fløibanen Funicular to Mount Fløyen for stunning city views and a hike.
- Afternoon: Visit the KODE Art Museums to admire Norwegian art and end your day with a stroll through the Bergen Botanical Garden.
- Evening: Experience Bergen's nightlife or enjoy a concert at the Grieg Hall.

Day 3: Norwegian Fjord Experience

- Day Trip: Book a fjord cruise to explore the majestic Sognefjord or Nærøyfjord, experiencing Norway's stunning natural beauty.
- Evening: Return to Bergen and relax with a casual dinner in the city centre.

Day 4: Bergen's Surrounding Nature

- Morning to Afternoon: Take a trip to Mount Ulriken and perhaps venture on the hike between Mount Ulriken and Mount Fløyen, known as Vidden.
- Evening: Dine at one of the mountain-top restaurants or return to the city for a more laid-back evening.

Day 5: Cultural Exploration

- Morning: Visit Troldhaugen, the home of composer Edvard Grieg.
- Afternoon: Explore the Old Bergen Museum or the Leprosy Museum for a dive into the city's history.
- Evening: Enjoy a traditional Norwegian meal at one of Bergen's historic restaurants.

Day 6: Adventure and Relaxation

- Morning to Afternoon: Choose an adventure like kayaking on the fjords, or for a more relaxed pace, visit the Bergen Aquarium.
- Evening: Spend your evening at Bryggen for shopping and dining, immersing yourself in the atmosphere of ancient Bergen.

Day 7: Day Trip Beyond Bergen

- Day Trip: Select a day trip to one of the nearby attractions, such as the Hardangerfjord, Flåm Railway, or the quaint coastal village of Rosendal.
- Evening: Return to Bergen for a farewell dinner, perhaps in one of the city's fine dining establishments, reflecting on a week well spent.

This itinerary offers a comprehensive experience of Bergen, from its historical roots and cultural richness to the breathtaking natural landscapes that surround it. Each day brings a new adventure, allowing travellers to immerse themselves fully in the beauty and diversity of Bergen and its environs.

CHAPTER 6

FOOD AND DINING

Here's a map direction to the top best restaurants in Bergen
https://shorturl.at/dtEQ4

6.1 Traditional Norwegian Cuisine

Traditional Norwegian cuisine offers a unique blend of ancient culinary traditions and fresh, locally-sourced ingredients, reflecting Norway's deep connection to its maritime, farming, and foraging heritage. Visitors to Bergen have the opportunity to explore a rich culinary landscape that encompasses everything from the sea to the mountains. Here's an extensive and comprehensive guide on traditional Norwegian dishes you must try and the best restaurants in Bergen where you can enjoy these delicacies.

Must-Try Traditional Norwegian Dishes:

Rakfisk

This fermented fish dish, typically made from trout, is a traditional Norwegian delicacy. The fermentation process gives it a strong flavour and it's usually served with flatbread, sour cream, and raw onions. It's an acquired taste but offers a genuine insight into historic Norwegian cuisine.

Fårikål

Fårikål, Norway's national dish, is a hearty mutton and cabbage stew, perfect for the colder months. It's simple, comforting, and deeply satisfying, showcasing the simplicity and purity of Norwegian flavours.

Kjøttkaker

Norwegian meatballs, or kjøttkaker, are larger and less spicy compared to their Swedish counterparts. They're usually served with mashed peas, potatoes, gravy, and lingonberry sauce, providing a comforting and homely meal.

Lutefisk

This lye-treated fish dish is another traditional Norwegian delicacy. Made from dried whitefish (commonly cod), lutefisk has a gelatinous texture and is typically served with boiled potatoes, mushy peas, and bacon.

Brunost

Brunost is a unique Norwegian brown cheese with a sweet, caramel-like taste. It's made from the whey of goat's milk, cow's milk, or a combination of both, and is a common topping on Norwegian open sandwiches.

Best Restaurants in Bergen for Traditional Norwegian Cuisine

Enhjørningen Fish Restaurant

Located at Bryggen, Enhjørningen offers an exquisite seafood dining experience. With its historic surroundings, the restaurant serves traditional dishes with a modern twist, making it a perfect spot to enjoy Norway's seafood treasures.

Bryggeloftet & Stuene

Also situated in the heart of Bryggen, Bryggeloftet & Stuene boasts a warm, traditional atmosphere. It's renowned for serving classic Norwegian dishes like fårikål, kjøttkaker, and locally sourced fish and game.

Cornelius Seafood Restaurant

Accessible by a boat trip from Bergen, Cornelius Seafood Restaurant on the island of Holmen is a must-visit for seafood lovers. The menu changes with the seasons, offering the freshest ingredients in a stunning fjord-side setting.

Lysverket

Focusing on modern Norwegian cuisine with an emphasis on sustainable seafood and local ingredients, Lysverket is a contemporary dining choice. It's located next to the KODE art museums, combining fine dining with artistic surroundings.

Bare Restaurant

Located in Bergen's opulent Bergen Børs Hotel, Bare is a fine dining restaurant that specialises in Nordic cuisine with a focus on organic and local ingredients. It's perfect for those looking to explore modern interpretations of traditional dishes.

Exploring traditional Norwegian cuisine in Bergen offers not just a taste of Norway's culinary heritage but also an immersive experience into the country's culture and traditions. Whether you're savouring the complex flavours of rakfisk, enjoying the homeliness of kjøttkaker, or indulging in the fresh catch at a seaside restaurant, Bergen's culinary scene is sure to leave a lasting impression.

6.2 Vegetarian and Vegan Options

Scan this barcode or click this link to make a table reservation and also access the map directions to these vegetarian and vegan options spread across Bergen **https://shorturl.at/bpCKX**

Bergen, with its picturesque landscapes and rich history, is also a haven for vegetarians and vegans, offering a delightful array of dining options that cater to plant-based diets. Recognizing the growing demand for vegetarian and vegan cuisine, many restaurants in Bergen have expanded their menus to include creative and delicious plant-based dishes. Here are five top recommendations for those seeking vegetarian and vegan dining experiences in Bergen:

1. Lysverket

Lysverket is renowned for its focus on sustainable and locally sourced ingredients, offering an innovative approach to Norwegian cuisine. While not exclusively vegetarian or vegan, Lysverket provides several plant-based options that are as inventive as they are flavorful. The restaurant's modern, airy space, located next to the KODE art museums, makes it a perfect spot for a special night out.

2. Pygmalion Økovarehus

For a cosy and casual dining experience, Pygmalion Økovarehus offers a variety of vegetarian and vegan dishes made with organic and locally sourced ingredients. This eco-friendly café not only serves excellent food but also doubles as a store selling eco-products. Its warm atmosphere and commitment to sustainability make it a favourite among locals and visitors alike.

3. Dwell

Dwell is a trendy restaurant that caters to a diverse crowd with its extensive vegetarian and vegan menu. From vegan burgers and pizzas to delicious salads and international dishes, Dwell proves that plant-based eating can be both satisfying and exciting. The restaurant's stylish interior and friendly service add to the overall dining experience.

4. Vegetarian House

A gem for plant-based diners, Vegetarian House offers a wide range of vegetarian and vegan dishes inspired by global cuisines. The menu features everything from Asian-inspired stir-fries and curries to classic Western dishes, all prepared with fresh, high-quality ingredients. The relaxed and welcoming environment makes it an ideal spot for a casual meal.

5. Norda

Located in the Clarion Hotel The Hub, Norda boasts a menu with a strong emphasis on local ingredients and sustainability. With several vegetarian and vegan options available, diners can enjoy beautifully prepared dishes that highlight the best of Norwegian produce. The restaurant's modern Nordic design and panoramic views of the city make it a must-visit for those looking for an upscale dining experience.

Bergen's culinary landscape is a testament to the city's innovative spirit and commitment to sustainability. Whether you're a strict vegetarian, vegan, or simply looking to explore plant-based dining, these five restaurants offer a taste of Bergen's diverse and delicious vegetarian and vegan cuisine.

To explore more options, make your reservation, and map directions to locate these restaurants, kindly scan the QR code or click the link provided above.

6.3 Seafood and Fish Markets

You can either scan this Qr code or click this link for map directions to seafood and food markets in Bergen https://rb.gy/r13m8g

Bergen, with its prime location on the western coast of Norway, is a paradise for seafood lovers. The city's long-standing maritime heritage and proximity to the cold, clear waters of the North Sea ensure a constant supply of fresh seafood, making it an essential part of local cuisine. Seafood and fish markets in Bergen offer not only a wide variety of fish and shellfish but also a glimpse into the city's cultural and culinary traditions.

The Bergen Fish Market (Fisketorget)

The heart of Bergen's seafood scene is the Bergen Fish Market (Fisketorget). Situated in the city centre by the harbour, this market has been a bustling hub of trade since the 12th century. Today, it continues to attract both locals and tourists with its vast array of fresh seafood, including salmon, cod, king crab, and the world-renowned Norwegian lobsters.

Visitors to the Fish Market will find not only raw seafood but also ready-to-eat dishes like fish soup, sushi, and seafood platters that can be enjoyed on the spot. The market also offers other Norwegian delicacies such as caviar, smoked salmon, and various fish roes. It's an ideal place to sample the freshness and quality of Norwegian seafood.

Fish Auctions and Wholesale

For those interested in the commercial side of the seafood industry, Bergen hosts fish auctions and wholesale operations that supply restaurants and markets across the country and internationally. These operations are typically not open to the public but play a crucial role in maintaining Norway's reputation for high-quality seafood.

Specialty Seafood Shops

Beyond the Fish Market, Bergen is home to specialty seafood shops that offer a curated selection of the finest seafood products. These shops pride themselves on their expertise and often provide rare delicacies not found in regular markets. They are perfect for gourmands looking to explore the depths of Norwegian seafood cuisine.

Seafood Dining in Bergen

Bergen's restaurants take full advantage of the city's access to fresh seafood, with many establishments featuring locally sourced fish and shellfish on their menus. From traditional Norwegian dishes such as "Bacalao" (salted cod stew) and "Gravlaks" (cured salmon) to contemporary international cuisines, dining in Bergen offers a chance to experience the best of Norway's seafood.

Sustainability and Tradition

In recent years, sustainability has become a key focus of the seafood industry in Bergen and Norway as a whole. Efforts are made to ensure that fishing practices are environmentally friendly and that fish populations are managed responsibly. This commitment to sustainability not only preserves Norway's fishing heritage but also ensures that future generations can enjoy the bounty of the sea.

Whether you're exploring the vibrant stalls of the Fish Market, enjoying a seafood feast at a local restaurant, or delving into the intricacies of seafood trade and sustainability, Bergen offers a rich and diverse seafood experience that is deeply rooted in the city's maritime history and culture.

6.4 Gourmet Restaurants and Local Eateries

Bergen, a culinary gem nestled between mountains and fjords, offers a diverse dining scene that caters to all tastes, from the sophisticated palate seeking gourmet experiences to the casual diner looking for authentic local eats. The city's rich culinary landscape is marked by a harmonious blend of traditional Norwegian cuisine and innovative gastronomy, making it a haven for food enthusiasts.

Gourmet Restaurants in Bergen

Lysverket

Lysverket, known for its modern approach to Norwegian cuisine, emphasises sustainable seafood and local ingredients. The restaurant, located next to the KODE art museums, offers a dining experience that is as aesthetically pleasing as it is delicious, with dishes that are both innovative and deeply rooted in Norwegian culinary traditions.

Bare Restaurant

Situated in the historic Bergen Børs Hotel, Bare Restaurant is at the forefront of the Nordic food revolution, offering an exquisite menu that changes with the seasons. The focus here is on purity, simplicity, and freshness, with ingredients sourced from the surrounding landscapes.

Cornelius Seafood Restaurant

Cornelius is one of Norway's best seafood restaurants, accessible by a short boat trip from Bergen. It offers a "Meteorological Menu," which changes daily based on the weather and available local ingredients, ensuring a unique and memorable dining experience with stunning fjord views.

Local Eateries in Bergen

Pingvinen

Pingvinen (The Penguin) is a cosy, laid-back pub and eatery offering traditional Norwegian comfort food. It's a favourite among locals for its relaxed atmosphere and hearty dishes such as meatballs, fish cakes, and the classic "fårikål" (lamb and cabbage stew).

Bryggeloftet & Stuene

Bryggeloftet & Stuene, located in the heart of the historic Bryggen area, serves traditional Norwegian cuisine in a warm, welcoming setting. With its picturesque views of the harbour and a menu featuring everything from fresh seafood to reindeer, it's an excellent spot for experiencing authentic local flavours.

Fish Me

Fish Me in the Bergen Fish Market offers a wide range of seafood in a more casual setting. Here, you can enjoy freshly prepared fish and shellfish dishes, sushi, and seafood platters, showcasing the best of what the Norwegian sea has to offer.

Culinary Diversity

Bergen's culinary scene is also marked by its international influences, with numerous eateries offering cuisines from around the world. This diversity ensures that visitors and locals alike can enjoy a global dining experience while savouring the tastes of Norway.

Whether you're dining at one of Bergen's gourmet restaurants, enjoying a meal at a local eatery, or exploring the city's international culinary offerings, Bergen promises an unforgettable dining experience that combines the best of Norwegian tradition and innovation.

6.5 Cafes and Bakeries

Bergen's cafes and bakeries are an integral part of the city's vibrant food scene, offering cosy retreats where locals and visitors alike can indulge in delicious baked goods, fresh coffee, and light meals. These establishments range from traditional bakeries that have been serving Bergen for generations to modern cafes that blend contemporary flavours with classic Norwegian baking traditions. Here's a glimpse into the warm and welcoming world of Bergen's cafes and bakeries.

Notable Cafes in Bergen

Det Lille Kaffekompaniet
Nestled near the entrance to Fløibanen Funicular, Det Lille Kaffekompaniet is Bergen's oldest specialty coffee shop.

Known for its intimate atmosphere and expertly brewed coffees, it's the perfect spot to relax after exploring the city. The cafe also offers a selection of homemade cakes and pastries, making it a favourite among those with a sweet tooth.

Kaf Kafe Bryggen

Situated in the historic Bryggen area, Kaf Kafe Bryggen is renowned for its cosy ambiance and excellent coffee. This charming cafe serves a variety of light meals and baked goods, including vegan and gluten-free options, ensuring there's something for everyone.

Blom

Blom is a modern café that prioritises sustainability and locally sourced ingredients. It's not just a place for coffee lovers but also a venue for cultural events, including live music and art exhibitions. Their menu features a range of organic teas, specialty coffees, and freshly baked pastries.

Beloved Bakeries in Bergen

Baker Brun

Baker Brun is one of Bergen's oldest bakeries, with a history stretching back over 100 years. Located in several spots across the city, including a quaint shop on Torgallmenningen, Baker Brun offers a wide range of traditional Norwegian bread, cakes, and pastries, such as the famous "skillingsbolle," a Bergen version of the cinnamon roll.

Godt Brød

Godt Brød is a chain of organic bakeries that focus on sustainability and high-quality ingredients. Their offerings include a variety of bread, sandwiches, and sweet treats. With several locations throughout Bergen, Godt Brød is a great place to enjoy a hearty breakfast or a nutritious lunch.

Colonialen Fetevarer
While primarily known as a delicatessen, Colonialen Fetevarer also operates a bakery that produces exquisite artisan bread and pastries. Located in the heart of Bergen, it's the go-to spot for those seeking high-quality, handcrafted baked goods.

Bergen's cafes and bakeries are more than just places to eat; they are community hubs where friends meet, travellers rest, and traditions continue to thrive. Whether you're in search of the perfect cup of coffee, a traditional Norwegian pastry, or a comfortable spot to unwind, Bergen's cafes and bakeries offer a warm welcome and a taste of local life.

CHAPTER 7

ARTS AND ENTERTAINMENT

7.1 Museums and Galleries

To explore Museums and Galleries in Bergen, know each of their operating days, time, entrance fees and a map directions to locate these Museums and Galleries, kindly scan the QR code or click the link provided beside. https://rb.gy/leyixs

Embarking on a cultural journey through Bergen, a city nestled between rain-swept hills and the deep, blue waters of the fjords, is akin to stepping into a living canvas, painted with the strokes of history, art, and maritime heritage. As your local guide, who has wandered through the cobbled streets, delved into the nooks and crannies of its museums, and basked in the glow of its galleries, I'm here to share with you the must-visit museums and galleries in Bergen that encapsulate the soul of this historic city.

The Hanseatic Museum and Schøtstuene - Time Travel to Medieval Bergen

Perched on the edge of Bryggen, the Hanseatic Museum is a gateway to the past, offering a glimpse into the lives of the German merchants from the Hanseatic League who lived and traded here from the 14th to the mid-17th century. The museum's creaking wooden floors, dimly lit rooms, and the authentic artefacts transport you to a time when Bergen was a bustling mercantile hub.

Don't miss the Schøtstuene, the assembly rooms with their large open hearths, where the merchants gathered to eat, conduct meetings, and stay warm during the frigid Norwegian winters.

KODE Art Museums - A Symphony of Nordic Art

KODE's collection of art museums along Lille Lungegårdsvann lake is a treasure trove of Nordic art, boasting over 50,000 pieces ranging from the Renaissance to contemporary works. KODE 3 shines a spotlight on the golden age of Norwegian art with masterpieces by Dahl, Astrup, and Munthe, and the largest collection of Edvard Munch's works outside of Oslo. KODE 4 focuses on modern and contemporary art, offering thought-provoking exhibitions that challenge and delight in equal measure.

The Bergen Maritime Museum - A Voyage Through Norway's Seafaring Legacy

Norway's profound connection with the sea is beautifully chronicled at the Bergen Maritime Museum. Through an impressive collection of ship models, maritime paintings, and navigational instruments, the museum narrates the story of Norway's adventures on the high seas, from the Viking Age to present-day oil explorations. The meticulously crafted models of Viking ships and the gripping tales of polar expeditions are particularly captivating.

Leprosy Museum - Unveiling Bergen's Compassionate Heart

Housed in the historic buildings of St. George's Hospital, the Leprosy Museum is a testament to Bergen's significant contributions to leprosy research. The museum offers a poignant look into the lives of the patients and the groundbreaking work of physicians like Armauer Hansen, who discovered the leprosy bacillus. It's a powerful reminder of the city's compassionate spirit and its pivotal role in medical history.

Bryggens Museum - Archaeological Wonders Beneath Your Feet

Built over the ruins discovered after a great fire in 1955, Bryggens Museum offers a fascinating archaeological insight into mediaeval Bergen. The preserved foundations beneath the museum floor tell tales of everyday life, trade, and the city's development over centuries. The museum serves as a compelling introduction to Bryggen's history before you walk through its iconic wooden alleyways.

Theta Museum - Bergen's Secret Resistance

Hidden away in a nondescript building on Bryggen's waterfront, the Theta Museum is a small but powerful tribute to the Norwegian resistance during World War II. The secret room, once used by the Theta Group to conduct clandestine radio operations, is preserved exactly as it was, offering an intimate glimpse into the bravery and ingenuity of those who fought against the occupation.

Art Galleries Galore - Bergen's Creative Pulse

Bergen's vibrant art scene is not confined to its museums. The city is dotted with galleries showcasing the work of local and international artists. The Galleri Allmenningen stands out with its focus on Norwegian and Nordic contemporary art, offering a mix of paintings, sculptures, and installations. No.5 Gallery, associated with KODE, often features avant-garde exhibitions that spark conversation and reflection.

Embarking on Your Cultural Exploration

As you meander through Bergen's streets, from the historic Bryggen to the serene Lille Lungegårdsvann, let each museum and gallery be a portal to a new understanding of this city's layered identity. Whether you're marvelling at a Munch masterpiece, pondering the legacy of the Hanseatic merchants, or reflecting on the resilience of humanity at the Leprosy Museum, Bergen's cultural institutions offer endless avenues for exploration and wonder.

In this city, every cobblestone has a story, and every gallery wall whispers tales of the North. As your guide, I've walked these paths, and felt the pulse of the city's rich heritage and vibrant art scene. Now, it's your turn to embark on this journey through Bergen's museums and galleries, where history, art, and the spirit of exploration converge in a beautiful symphony. Welcome to Bergen, where every visit is a voyage through time and imagination.

7.2 Theater and Performances

The vibrant city of Bergen, Norway, is not just known for its picturesque landscapes and historic sites but also for its thriving theatre and performance scene. This cultural hub offers a rich tapestry of theatrical experiences that cater to a wide array of tastes, from traditional plays and musicals to avant-garde performances and international festivals. Let's delve into the heart of Bergen's theatre and performance scene, exploring the key venues that contribute to its dynamic cultural life.

Den Nationale Scene

Located at Engen 1, Den Nationale Scene stands as one of Norway's oldest permanent theatres, established in 1850. This prestigious venue is steeped in history, having been the stage for early works of the world-renowned playwright Henrik Ibsen. Today, it continues to be a cornerstone of Norwegian theatre, presenting a diverse repertoire that includes classic Norwegian and international plays, modern dramas, and musicals. The theatre's stunning architecture and rich programming make it a must-visit for theatre enthusiasts exploring Bergen.

Bergen International Festival

Annually transforming the city into a vibrant cultural melting pot, the Bergen International Festival showcases a wide range of performances from theatre and dance to music and opera. Various venues across the city, including the Grieg Hall at Edvard Griegs pass 1 and the Bergenhus Fortress, become stages for this grand celebration of the arts. The festival not only highlights Norwegian performers but also features international artists, making it a pivotal event in Bergen's cultural calendar.

BIT Teatergarasjen

For those interested in contemporary and experimental theatre, BIT Teatergarasjen is a beacon of avant-garde and cutting-edge performances. Located at Nøstegaten 54, this venue is known for its innovative programming, which includes new theatre works, contemporary dance, and performance art. BIT Teatergarasjen also organises the annual Oktoberdans and Meteor Festival, further cementing its role as a key player in Bergen's avant-garde scene.

Logen Teater

Situated at Øvre Ole Bulls plass 6, Logen Teater is a historic venue with a cosy atmosphere, offering a more intimate setting for performances. This charming theatre hosts a variety of events, including concerts, stand-up comedy, and small-scale theatrical productions. Its central location and eclectic programming make Logen Teater a beloved spot among locals and visitors alike.

Cornerteateret

Cornerteateret, located in Kong Christian Frederiks plass 4, is Bergen's hub for independent theatre groups and artists. This venue provides a platform for innovative and experimental work, supporting the development of new Norwegian and international theatre. With its commitment to fostering artistic diversity, Cornerteateret is a key figure in nurturing the next generation of theatre talent in Bergen.

Bergen and Beyond

The city's passion for theatre and performances extends beyond these venues, with numerous smaller stages and community theatres contributing to Bergen's vibrant cultural landscape. From the traditional to the experimental, Bergen's theatres reflect the city's rich artistic heritage and its forward-looking approach to the arts.

Exploring Bergen's theatre and performance scene offers a unique insight into the city's cultural heartbeat, where the power of storytelling and artistic expression brings people together. Whether you're a fan of classic dramas, contemporary performances, or anything in between, Bergen's stages offer a world of experiences waiting to be discovered.

7.3 Music and Nightlife

Bergen, often hailed as the gateway to the fjords, is not just renowned for its stunning landscapes but also for its vibrant music scene and electrifying nightlife. This city, with its rich maritime history and artistic heritage, is a breeding ground for musical talent and a hub for nightlife enthusiasts. From intimate jazz clubs to bustling nightclubs, Bergen offers a multitude of venues that cater to every taste, ensuring that the city's cultural pulse beats as strongly at night as it does by day.

Live Music Venues and Their Rich Offerings

USF Verftet (Georgernes Verft 12) is an absolute cornerstone of Bergen's music scene. Located in a converted sardine factory, this multi-purpose cultural venue hosts an array of concerts ranging from rock and indie to electronic and experimental music. Its industrial charm and seaside location make it a unique spot to experience live performances.

Bergen Live organises concerts and events featuring international stars and local talent across various venues, including the iconic Bergenhus Fortress. This historic site transforms into an open-air concert venue, providing unforgettable live music experiences against the backdrop of mediaeval stone walls and the adjacent harbour.

Ole Bull Scene (Øvre Ole Bulls plass 3) offers a diverse program of events, from concerts to theatre productions, in the heart of the city. Named after the famous Norwegian violinist Ole Bull, this venue upholds a tradition of celebrating musical excellence.

Victoria Café & Pub (Nedre Korskirkeallmenningen 1A) is renowned for its cosy atmosphere and regular jazz nights. It's a favourite among locals and tourists alike who are looking to enjoy quality live jazz in a relaxed, friendly setting.

Nightclubs and Bars - The Heartbeat of Bergen's Nightlife

Landmark (Rasmus Meyers allé 5), located within the Bergen Kunsthall, is not just an art space but also a popular nightclub and café. Known for its eclectic events ranging from DJ sets to art exhibitions, Landmark is where Bergen's artistic and nocturnal scenes collide.

Metro Nightclub (Vaskerelven 6), one of Bergen's most popular dance clubs, offers an energetic atmosphere with a diverse music policy that includes everything from chart-toppers to electronic beats. It's the place to be for those looking to dance the night away.

No Stress (Hollendergaten 11) offers a slightly different nightlife experience, focusing on high-quality cocktails in a relaxed, stress-free environment. Its vintage decor and extensive cocktail menu make it a perfect spot for a night out with friends.

The Bergen Music Festival Scene

Bergen's music scene is further enriched by its festivals, with Bergenfest being a highlight. Held annually at Bergenhus Fortress, this festival showcases a wide range of genres, including rock, pop, indie, and electronic music, attracting both international acts and local stars.

Nattjazz, one of Europe's longest-running jazz festivals, takes place at various venues around the city, including USF Verftet. It's a celebration of jazz in all its forms, from traditional to contemporary, featuring Norwegian and international artists.

Conclusion

Music and nightlife in Bergen offer an immersive cultural experience, reflecting the city's diverse artistic spirit. From historic venues hosting live concerts to modern nightclubs pulsing with electronic beats, Bergen's nightlife promises memorable experiences for every visitor. Whether you're a passionate music lover or just looking to enjoy a night out on the town, Bergen's vibrant scene is sure to captivate and entertain.

7.4 Festivals and Events in 2024

Bergen, known affectionately as the gateway to the fjords, is a city that pulsates with life all year round, offering a dynamic array of festivals and events that cater to every interest and passion. Whether you're drawn by the allure of music, the excitement of cultural celebrations, or the charm of traditional Norwegian festivities, Bergen in 2024 promises an enriching calendar that I, as a local guide author and a seasoned wanderer of its historic streets and scenic landscapes, am thrilled to share with you.

Bergen International Festival (Festspillene i Bergen), held in late May to early June, stands as a testament to Bergen's rich cultural tapestry. This festival is Scandinavia's largest celebration of art and culture, showcasing everything from music, theatre, dance, opera, and visual art. The city comes alive with performances set in various venues, including the historic Grieg Hall, picturesque outdoor settings, and intimate, hidden stages throughout the city. It's a feast for the senses, offering experiences that range from avant-garde productions to classical performances that resonate with the city's historical ambiance.

Bergenfest, following closely on the heels of the International Festival, transforms the mediaeval fortress of Bergenhus into a sprawling venue for music lovers. Spanning several days in June, this festival is a vibrant celebration of rock, pop, and electronic music, attracting both international stars and emerging talents. As you wander from stage to stage, the air is electric with melodies, and the backdrop of Bergen's waterfront adds a magical touch to every performance.

For those with a penchant for the cinematic arts, Bergen International Film Festival (BIFF) in October is a must-visit. As Norway's largest film festival, BIFF presents a curated selection of global cinema, from thought-provoking documentaries to groundbreaking feature films. It's a gathering that offers not just entertainment, but also profound insights into diverse cultures and perspectives, echoing the city's seafaring heritage that has always connected Bergen to the wider world.

Culinary enthusiasts will revel in the Bergen Food Festival (Bergen Matfestival), held in September. This event is a heartfelt ode to the bounty of the region, showcasing the best of local produce, seafood, and culinary traditions. Walking through the festival, you'll encounter passionate producers, chefs, and locals, each sharing stories and flavours that are a testament to Norway's rich gastronomic heritage. It's an opportunity not just to taste but to learn about the sustainable practices and the love of land and sea that define Norwegian cuisine.

As the year winds down, the Bergen Christmas Market and Festival of Lights bring a cosy, festive atmosphere to the city's already picturesque setting. The Christmas market, set up in the heart of Bergen, offers a maze of stalls brimming with Norwegian handicrafts, seasonal treats, and warming drinks. The Festival of Lights, typically held in November, is a captivating event where thousands of lights illuminate the city, marking the beginning of the holiday season. It's a time of community, warmth, and joy, reflective of the city's spirit.

Pepperkakebyen, the world's largest gingerbread city, is another highlight of the festive season. Created anew each year by volunteers, this edible wonderland features replicas of Bergen's famous buildings and landmarks, all crafted from gingerbread. It's a delightful exhibition that captures the imagination of young and old alike, reminding everyone of the magic that pervades Bergen during the winter months.

Amid these marquee events, Bergen's cultural calendar is dotted with numerous other celebrations, from jazz festivals and literature events to traditional Norwegian folk festivals that offer a glimpse into the country's soul. Each event is an invitation to immerse yourself in the life of the city, to meet its people, and to create memories that resonate with the spirit of exploration and discovery.

As a local guide author who has wandered through Bergen's cobblestone streets, soaked in its rain-drenched beauty, and celebrated alongside its warm, welcoming inhabitants, I assure you that Bergen's festivals and events in 2024 are not just occasions to mark on your calendar. They are experiences to be lived, cherished, and remembered. Whether you find yourself swaying to the rhythm of a concert at Bergenfest, pondering the nuances of a film at BIFF, or savouring a bite of fresh, local fare at the Food Festival, you're partaking in the ongoing story of a city that, despite its modest size, has a heart as vast and deep as the fjords that embrace it.

7.5 Local Artisan Shops and Souvenirs

I've been fortunate to explore the nooks and crannies of this picturesque city, unearthing spots that celebrate the spirit of Bergen through their artisanal creations and souvenirs. Let me guide you through some of the city's best-kept secrets, where the essence of Bergen's rich cultural heritage and natural beauty is encapsulated in each carefully crafted piece.

Bryggen's Handicraft Market is a must-visit for anyone seeking authentic Bergen craftsmanship. Nestled within the historic wharf of Bryggen, a UNESCO World Heritage Site, this market brims with life and creativity. Local artisans display their work with pride, offering everything from hand-knitted sweaters that promise to keep the chill at bay, to delicate silver jewellery inspired by Norse mythology and the rugged Norwegian landscape. Each stall tells a story, inviting you to bring home a piece of Bergen's history and artistry.

Det Lille Kaffekompaniet is not only Bergen's oldest coffee shop but also a treasure trove of local flavours. Beyond its aromatic brews, the shop offers beautifully packaged Norwegian chocolates and coffee beans that make for perfect souvenirs. Tucked away in a narrow alley, this cosy spot is an ideal place to savour the local vibe and pick up a treat that captures the essence of Bergen's cafe culture.

Bergen Glassblower (Bergens Glassblåseri) is where the magic of glassblowing comes to life. Watching the glassblower at work is a mesmerising experience, transforming molten glass into exquisite pieces that range from vibrant vases to intricate ornaments. Each piece reflects the colours and light of Bergen's seascape, making them unique keepsakes that carry the spirit of the city.

Tveit Tunet, located just a short trip from the city centre, is a haven for traditional Norwegian crafts. This family-run farm and workshop specialises in woollen products, from cosy mittens to soft blankets, all made from the wool of sheep grazing in the surrounding landscapes. It's a place where the connection to nature and heritage is woven into every thread, offering souvenirs that embody the warmth and simplicity of Norwegian country life.

Fjord Shop presents a curated collection of Norwegian design, with a focus on sustainability and local materials. From elegant wooden serving boards shaped like the fjords themselves to minimalist jewellery echoing Scandinavian aesthetics, the shop offers a modern take on Norwegian traditions. It's an ideal spot for those looking to bring home a piece of Bergen that blends contemporary design with timeless craftsmanship.

The Bergen Market, located in the heart of the city, is not just a place to savour local delicacies but also a great spot to find edible souvenirs. Here, you can pick up traditional Norwegian brown cheese, locally smoked salmon, or handmade chocolates. Each stall offers a taste of the region's bounty, allowing you to bring the flavours of Bergen to your own kitchen.

Oleana, a short journey from Bergen's centre, is a textile factory and shop where beauty and ethics intertwine. Known for their vibrant, patterned knitwear, Oleana's products are a testament to sustainable production and impeccable Norwegian design. A visit to their factory offers insight into the meticulous craftsmanship behind each garment, making any purchase a meaningful and stylish reminder of your visit to Bergen.

Exploring Bergen's artisan shops and markets is an adventure in itself, offering a glimpse into the city's creative heart and soul. These local treasures not only serve as mementos of your travels but also as a way to support the artisans and traditions that make Bergen so special. Whether you're drawn to the warmth of hand-knitted wool, the sparkle of blown glass, or the rich flavours of Norwegian cuisine, Bergen's local artisan shops and souvenirs promise to provide a tangible connection to the city's vibrant culture and stunning natural beauty.

CHAPTER 8

SHOPPING AND LEISURE

Go on any of your shopping by scanning this barcode or click this link https://rb.gy/gcjwxp for a map guide.

8.1 Shopping Districts and Malls

Recommended Shopping Malls and Centers in Bergen

1. Bergen Storsenter
    - Location: Strømgaten 8, Bergen
    - Highlights: As the largest shopping centre in the heart of Bergen, adjacent to the Bergen railway station, Bergen Storsenter boasts over 70 stores. It offers a wide range of products from fashion and beauty to electronics and home goods. The mall also houses several cafes and eateries.

2. Xhibition Shopping Center
    - Location: Småstrandgaten 3, Bergen
    - Highlights: With its modern architectural design, Xhibition offers a diverse selection of shops and services, including fashion boutiques, home decor, health and beauty stores, as well as dining options. It's known for its convenient location and the rooftop restaurant with views of the city.

3. Kløverhuset
    - Location: Strandgaten 13-15, Bergen
    - Highlights: The oldest shopping centre in Bergen, Kløverhuset, is situated on the historic Bryggen waterfront. It offers a mix of high-end fashion brands, beauty products, and unique gifts. The top floor has a restaurant that provides stunning views of the harbour.

4. Galleriet
    - Location: Torgallmenningen 8, Bergen
    - Highlights: Located in the bustling city square Torgallmenningen, Galleriet is one of Bergen's most fashionable shopping destinations. It houses a wide array of stores, from Norwegian design and fashion to international brands, alongside cafes and restaurants.
5. Lagunen Storsenter
    - Location: Laguneveien 1, Rådal
    - Highlights: Situated a bit outside the city centre, Lagunen Storsenter is one of the largest shopping centres in Norway. It offers an extensive range of shops, including clothing, electronics, and groceries, as well as numerous services and dining options. Easily accessible by bus or car.
6. Åsane Storsenter
    - Location: Bygg G, Åsane Senter 42, Nyborg
    - Highlights: Located in the Åsane district, this shopping centre is known for its variety of shops catering to all family needs, including fashion, sports equipment, electronics, and home decor. The centre also includes several restaurants and a play area for children.

Practical Tips for Shopping in Bergen

- Transportation: Most shopping centres in Bergen are easily accessible by public transport (bus and Bybanen, the light rail). Free parking is often available for visitors driving to the malls outside the city centre.
- Currency & Payments: Norway uses the Norwegian Krone (NOK). Credit cards are widely accepted, but it's advisable to have some cash for smaller purchases, especially in markets or smaller shops.
- Tax-Free Shopping: Tourists from outside the EU can benefit from tax-free shopping in Norway, allowing for a refund on the value-added tax (VAT) for purchases above a certain amount. Look for the "Tax-Free" logo and ask in-store for details.

These shopping centres in Bergen provide not just a wide range of shopping options but also a glimpse into the local culture and the convenience of modern amenities, making your visit to Bergen a memorable experience.

8.2 Local Markets and Specialty Stores

https://rb.gy/a64hb3 click this link or scan the code to go on a local markets and specialty stores exploration.

Exploring local markets and specialty stores in Bergen offers a unique glimpse into the city's culture and the opportunity to find distinctive goods and souvenirs. These markets and stores cater to a variety of interests, from local food specialties to handcrafted items, making them essential stops for visitors seeking authentic Norwegian experiences.

Local Markets in Bergen

1. Fish Market (Fisketorget)
    - Location: Torget, Bergen
    - Highlights: Situated in the heart of Bergen, the Fish Market is one of Norway's most famous outdoor markets. It's not only a place to buy fresh seafood, fruits, and vegetables but also a cultural landmark where you can taste local delicacies like smoked salmon, caviar, and king crab. The market also features stands selling Norwegian crafts and souvenirs.
2. Bryggen Handelssted
    - Location: Bryggen, Bergen

- Highlights: Located in the historic Bryggen area, this market area is known for its artisan shops and studios. Here, you can find handcrafted items, traditional Norwegian knitted sweaters, and unique jewellery. It's an excellent place for those looking to bring home a piece of Bergen's heritage.

3. Festplassen Market
    - Location: Festplassen, Bergen
    - Highlights: Occasionally, Festplassen becomes home to various markets, including book fairs, antique markets, and Christmas markets. These events are perfect for finding unique items and enjoying the festive atmosphere.

Specialty Stores in Bergen

1. Oleana
    - Location: Strandkaien 2A, Bergen
    - Highlights: Oleana is a Norwegian brand known for its high-quality woollen textiles and knitwear, combining traditional Norwegian patterns with contemporary designs. Their flagship store in Bergen offers a wide range of sweaters, dresses, and accessories.
2. Troll Shop
    - Location: Bryggen, Bergen
    - Highlights: The Troll Shop is dedicated to all things troll-related, offering a fun selection of Norwegian troll figurines, postcards, and souvenirs. It's a quirky and memorable shop located in the historic Bryggen district.
3. Det Lille Kaffekompaniet
    - Location: Nedre Fjellsmauet 2, Bergen
    - Highlights: Known as Bergen's oldest coffee shop, this place is a must-visit for coffee enthusiasts. They offer a selection of high-quality beans, brewing equipment, and delicious homemade cakes. The cosy atmosphere makes it a perfect spot for a relaxing break.

4. Bergen Bookstore (Bergen Bokhandel)
    - Location: Fjøsangerveien 70, Bergen
    - Highlights: This independent bookstore offers a wide selection of English and Norwegian books, including local history, literature, and travel guides. It's an ideal place for book lovers looking to discover Norwegian authors or find travel inspiration.

Tips for Shopping in Local Markets and Specialty Stores

- Cash and Cards: While most vendors accept credit cards, having some cash on hand is useful for smaller purchases or in places where cards might not be accepted.
- Opening Hours: Markets and specialty stores may have varying opening hours, especially on weekends. Check in advance to plan your visit.
- Language: Most vendors speak English, so don't hesitate to ask questions or for recommendations.

Exploring Bergen's local markets and specialty stores is not only about shopping; it's an adventure into the heart of Norwegian culture and tradition. Whether you're looking for unique gifts, tasty treats, or a piece of Bergen to take home with you, these markets and stores offer something special for every visitor.

8.3 Handcrafted Goods and Antiques

In Bergen, the search for handcrafted goods and antiques can lead you through quaint cobblestone streets, historic districts, and charming boutiques, offering a unique blend of the city's rich heritage and contemporary craftsmanship. Here's a guide to discovering these treasures, ensuring your shopping experience in Bergen is as fulfilling as it is memorable.

Handcrafted Goods in Bergen

Bryggen Handelssted

- Overview: Nestled in the iconic Bryggen wharf, a UNESCO World Heritage site, this area is famed for its artisan shops. You can find everything from traditional Norwegian knitwear and handcrafted silver jewellery to bespoke ceramics and glass work, all made by local artisans.
- What to Buy: Look for intricately patterned Norwegian sweaters, Sami-inspired silver jewellery, and hand-painted ceramics that reflect Norway's natural beauty.

Bergen Husfliden

- Location: Vetrlidsallmenningen 2, Bergen
- Overview: This shop specialises in Norwegian crafts and traditional costumes (Bunads). It's a great place to find authentic handcrafted goods, textiles, and woodwork.
- What to Buy: Traditional Norwegian Bunads, wooden kitchen utensils, woven rugs, and hand-knitted mittens are perfect souvenirs.

Antiques and Vintage Finds in Bergen

Lille Lerke

- Location: Fjøsangerveien 30 A, Bergen
- Overview: A charming antique shop offering a carefully curated selection of vintage furniture, decor items, and Norwegian collectibles. Each piece tells a story of Norway's past.
- What to Buy: Vintage Norwegian pottery, antique furniture pieces, and retro Norwegian home accessories.

Skostredet

- Overview: This vibrant street in the heart of Bergen is known for its eclectic mix of small, independent shops, including several vintage and second-hand stores. It's the perfect place to hunt for unique finds and antiques.
- What to Buy: Vintage clothing, second-hand books, retro Norwegian design items, and vinyl records.

Shopping Tips for Handcrafted Goods and Antiques

- Authenticity: When shopping for handcrafted goods, look for signs or certifications of authenticity, especially for items like Bunads or Sami crafts. This ensures you're purchasing a genuine piece of Norwegian culture.
- Negotiation: While prices for handcrafted goods are usually fixed, there might be some room for negotiation at antique shops or flea markets. Don't be afraid to politely ask if the price is flexible.
- Condition: Always inspect antiques or vintage items for condition. Minor imperfections can add character, but you should be aware of any significant damage that could affect the item's value or usability.
- Shipping: For larger antique finds, inquire about shipping options. Many shops can arrange for international shipping, ensuring your treasures make it home safely.

Exploring Bergen's offerings of handcrafted goods and antiques not only enriches your shopping experience but also offers a deeper connection to Norwegian culture and history. Whether you're looking for a special gift, a unique piece of jewellery, or a vintage decor item, Bergen's shops and markets provide a treasure trove of possibilities waiting to be discovered.

8.4 Fashion Boutiques and Designer Stores

When visiting Bergen, a city renowned for its stunning natural beauty and rich cultural heritage, fashion enthusiasts will find a treasure trove of unique shopping experiences. The city's fashion boutiques and designer stores offer a distinct blend of Scandinavian minimalism, cutting-edge design, and traditional Norwegian craftsmanship. To navigate Bergen's fashion scene like a pro, follow this guide on exploring the city's fashion boutiques and designer stores, ensuring a shopping experience that's as memorable as it is stylish.

Start with Bryggen and the City Center

Begin your fashion journey in the heart of Bergen, starting with the historic Bryggen area. This UNESCO World Heritage Site is not only a testament to the city's Hanseatic history but also home to a number of quaint boutiques featuring Norwegian designs and handcrafted accessories. Wander the narrow alleyways to discover unique pieces that blend tradition with contemporary style.

After exploring Bryggen, make your way to the city centre and Torgallmenningen, Bergen's main square. Here, you'll find a mix of high-street brands and independent boutiques. The city centre is compact and easily walkable, making it a pleasure to explore on foot.

Seek Out Local Designers

One of the highlights of shopping in Bergen is the opportunity to explore the works of local Norwegian and Scandinavian designers. Stores like Norwegian Rain and T-Michael are known for their innovative outerwear that doesn't compromise on style or functionality, perfect for Bergen's rainy climate. These shops not only offer high-quality garments but also a chance to take home a piece of Bergen's design ethos.

Discover Fashion Boutiques

Bergen is dotted with small, independent fashion boutiques that offer curated collections of clothing, jewellery, and accessories. Shops like Pepper, Lot333, and Ensemble offer a range of styles from Scandinavian chic to international trends. These boutiques are perfect for finding unique pieces that aren't available in larger retail chains. The staff in these stores are often very knowledgeable and can offer personalised styling advice.

Explore Strandgaten and Skostredet

Strandgaten, one of Bergen's main shopping streets, and the nearby Skostredet, known for its vibrant atmosphere and eclectic shops, are must-visits for any fashion enthusiast. These areas are home to a mix of fashion boutiques, second-hand stores, and designer shops. Skostredet, in particular, has a youthful vibe with its array of vintage shops, independent labels, and cosy cafes — perfect for a shopping break.

Tips for a Successful Shopping Experience

- Timing: Most shops in Bergen open around 10 am and close by 5 pm on weekdays, with shorter hours on Saturdays. Plan your shopping trip accordingly, and note that many stores are closed on Sundays.
- Weather: Bergen is known for its rainy weather, so pack an umbrella or a waterproof jacket to stay comfortable while hopping from shop to shop.
- Currency and Payments: Norway uses the Norwegian Krone (NOK). While most places accept major credit cards, it's a good idea to have some cash on hand for smaller boutiques or market purchases.
- Tax-Free Shopping: If you're visiting from outside Norway, you may be eligible for a tax refund on your purchases. Look for stores that offer Tax-Free Shopping and remember to keep your receipts for the refund process at the airport.

8.5 Spas and Wellness Centers

Whether it's after a day of exploring the city's historic sites or before embarking on an adventure in the surrounding fjords, Bergen's wellness offerings cater to a variety of needs, from luxurious spa treatments to holistic wellness experiences. This guide will help you navigate the best spas and wellness centres in Bergen, ensuring a tranquil and restorative experience during your visit.

Vulkana Spa

Overview: Originally a fishing vessel, Vulkana has been transformed into a unique floating spa experience. It offers a combination of traditional Scandinavian spa treatments and the unparalleled beauty of Norwegian nature.

Treatments: Guests can enjoy the wood-fired sauna, a refreshing dip in the ocean, the mineral-rich saltwater hot tub on deck, and a hammam that promises relaxation and rejuvenation.

Special Features: Vulkana also offers tailored spa cruises around the stunning fjords, where you can immerse yourself in the tranquillity of Norway's natural landscapes while indulging in luxurious spa treatments.

The Well

Overview: Situated in the heart of Bergen, The Well is one of the city's premier wellness centres, known for its comprehensive approach to health and relaxation.

Treatments: It features a wide range of facilities, including saunas, steam baths, therapy pools, and relaxation areas. The Well specialises in treatments that integrate ancient traditions with modern wellness techniques, including massages, facials, and body treatments.

Special Features: The Well is also known for its wellness workshops and classes, such as yoga and meditation, designed to enhance your wellbeing beyond the physical treatments.

Bergen Hammam

Overview: Drawing inspiration from the traditional Turkish hammam, Bergen Hammam offers a unique spa experience in the city. It's a place where guests can enjoy the benefits of steam baths and professional exfoliation treatments in a warm and inviting atmosphere.

Treatments: The Hammam experience includes a body scrub using a Kese mitt, followed by a foam massage and a series of warm and cold baths. Guests can also opt for additional treatments like clay masks and aromatherapy massages.

Special Features: Bergen Hammam places a strong emphasis on community and relaxation, providing a social space where guests can relax and rejuvenate together.

Solstrand Hotel & Bad

Overview: Located just outside Bergen, Solstrand Hotel & Bad offers breathtaking views of the fjords and mountains, making it an ideal retreat for those seeking peace and relaxation in a stunning natural setting.

Treatments: The spa at Solstrand features outdoor and indoor pools, saunas, and a fitness room. It offers a range of treatments, including massages, facials, and body wraps, using natural and organic skincare products.

Special Features: Guests can take advantage of the hotel's location by combining spa visits with outdoor activities such as hiking, kayaking, or simply enjoying the panoramic views of the fjords.

Tips for Visiting Spas and Wellness Centers in Bergen

- Book in Advance: To ensure availability, especially during peak seasons, it's wise to book your treatments or spa days in advance.
- Inquire About Packages: Many spas offer packages that include multiple treatments at a reduced price, providing a more comprehensive wellness experience.

- Check for Special Requirements: Some spas may have specific guidelines or requirements, such as age limits or health considerations. It's best to check these details before your visit.
- Relax and Unwind: Remember, the goal of visiting a spa or wellness centre is to relax and rejuvenate. Allow yourself to fully embrace the experience and the serene environment.

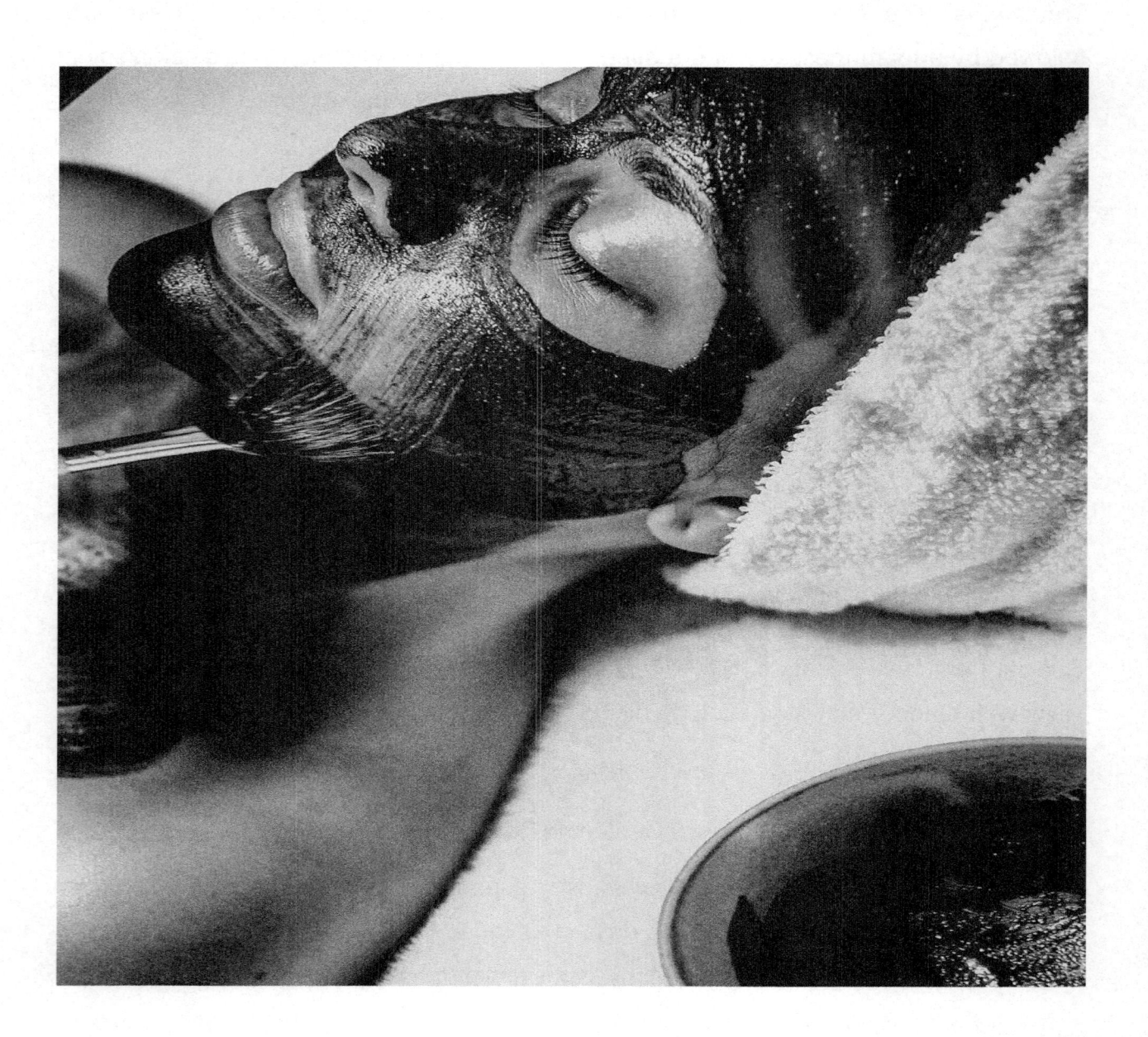

CHAPTER 9

OUTDOOR ADVENTURES

For all outdoors activities and adventures in Bergen, kindly scan this code or click this link **https://rb.gy/q96tha**, for your map guide to each of them.

9.1 Hiking and Nature Trails

Bergen, often referred to as the gateway to the fjords of Norway, is a city that boasts an exceptional natural landscape, making it a haven for outdoor enthusiasts and hikers. The city is surrounded by seven mountains, each offering a variety of trails that cater to all levels of expertise, from leisurely walks to challenging hikes. In this essay, we will explore the best areas for hiking and nature trails in Bergen, providing essential information to help visitors make the most of their outdoor adventures.

One of the most accessible and popular hiking destinations in Bergen is **Mount Fløyen.** Known for its panoramic views of the city, the fjord, and the surrounding mountains, Mount Fløyen is a must-visit for anyone looking to experience Bergen's natural beauty. There are several trails to choose from, including the gentle hike to **Brushytten**, which is approximately 2.5 km one way and suitable for families. For those seeking a more adventurous hike, the trail extending from **Fløyen to Rundemanen** and further to **Mount Ulriken** offers stunning vistas and a more challenging experience. The quickest way to reach the top of Mount Fløyen is by taking the **Fløibanen funicular** from the city centre, but for those who prefer to hike, there are several paths starting from the city centre that take about 45 minutes to an hour to reach the top.

Mount Ulriken, the highest of Bergen's seven mountains, offers some of the most challenging and rewarding hikes. The summit provides a spectacular panorama of the city, the sea, and the surrounding peaks. The **Vidden Trail**, which connects **Mount Ulriken to Mount Fløyen, is a 13 km hike across the mountain plateau called "Vidden,"** offering breathtaking views and taking about 4-6 hours to complete. Another demanding hike is the trail from **Ulriken to Løvstakken**, a 15 km trail that takes hikers through diverse landscapes, including forests, marshes, and rocky terrain. The easiest way to reach the summit of Mount Ulriken is by taking the **Ulriksbanen cable car**, but there are also several hiking trails leading up to the mountain.

For those looking for a more leisurely stroll or a light hike, **Løvstien** is a scenic walking and biking path that stretches from the city centre to the foothills of Løvstakken mountain. The path is approximately 5 km long and takes you through residential areas, forests, and along a beautiful lake, making it perfect for a relaxed walk.

Stoltzekleiven is another popular hiking spot in Bergen, known for its steep and challenging trail. The trail is famous for its annual "**Stoltzekleiven Opp**" race and is a short but intense hike, leading up stone steps to the top of **Sandviksfjellet mountain**. The trail is only 0.8 km long but ascends over 300 metres with more than 700 steps, making it a strenuous climb that rewards hikers with stunning views from the top.

Lastly, the **Nordnes Peninsula** offers a more urban hiking experience, with a mix of natural beauty and cultural sights. The gentle walk from **Nordnes Park to Nyhavn** is a great way to explore the area, offering views of the harbour, historical buildings, and the Bergen Aquarium along the way.

In conclusion, Bergen's diverse landscape provides a wide range of hiking and nature trail experiences, from gentle walks to challenging mountain hikes. Whether you're a seasoned hiker or just looking for a leisurely stroll, Bergen has something to offer for everyone. It's important to check the weather forecast, wear appropriate clothing and footwear, and bring water and snacks for your adventure. With its stunning natural beauty and variety of trails, Bergen is a true paradise for hiking enthusiasts.

9.2 Cycling Routes and Bike Rentals

Bergen, with its picturesque landscapes and well-maintained cycling routes, is an ideal destination for biking enthusiasts. Whether you're a seasoned cyclist or a casual rider, the city and its surroundings offer a variety of routes that cater to different skill levels and preferences. In this section, we'll explore some of the best cycling routes in Bergen and provide information on bike rentals to help you plan your cycling adventure.

Cycling Routes in Bergen

1. **Bergen City Center to Nordnes Peninsula**
   - Distance: Approximately 5 km (round trip)
   - Difficulty: Easy
   - Description: This leisurely route takes you through the historic streets of Bergen's city centre, along the picturesque waterfront, and out to the Nordnes Peninsula. It's perfect for a relaxed ride with plenty of opportunities to stop and explore Bergen's cultural attractions.

2. **Fjellveien**
   - Distance: Approximately 3 km (one way)
   - Difficulty: Easy to Moderate
   - Description: Fjellveien is a scenic road that runs along the mountainside above Bergen's city centre, offering stunning views of the city and the surrounding fjords. The route is relatively flat and suitable for cyclists of all levels.

3. **Bergen to Fantoft Stave Church**
   - Distance: Approximately 10 km (round trip)
   - Difficulty: Moderate

- Description: This route takes you from the city centre to the historic Fantoft Stave Church, passing through residential areas and green spaces. The ride is mostly flat with some gentle hills, making it suitable for intermediate cyclists.

4. **Rallarvegen (The Navvies Road)**

- Distance: Up to 80 km (one way)
- Difficulty: Moderate to Challenging
- Description: For a more adventurous ride, consider tackling a section of the famous Rallarvegen, which stretches from the mountainous region of Haugastøl to Flåm. This route offers breathtaking views of the Norwegian landscape, including mountains, waterfalls, and valleys. The terrain can be challenging, so it's best suited for experienced cyclists.

Bike Rentals in Bergen

To explore Bergen on two wheels, you can rent a bike from various outlets in the city. Here are some options:

1. **Bergen Bysykkel (Bergen City Bike)**

- Website: Bergen Bysykkel
- Description: Bergen Bysykkel offers a convenient bike-sharing service with numerous docking stations around the city. You can use their app to find a bike, unlock it, and start your ride. It's an excellent option for short trips within the city.

2. **Bergen Bike Rent**

- Adresse: Strandkaien 3, 5013 Bergen
- Website: Bergen Bike Rent
- Description: Located near the Fish Market, Bergen Bike Rent offers a variety of bicycles for rent, including city bikes, road bikes, and electric bikes. They also provide helmets and other accessories.

3. **Bike the Fjords**
    - Address: Dreggs Almenningen 1, 5003 Bergen
    - Website: Bike the Fjords
    - Description: Bike the Fjords specialises in guided bike tours and bike rentals for those looking to explore the fjords and mountains around Bergen. They offer a range of bikes, including e-bikes and touring bikes, to suit different terrains and preferences.

In conclusion, Bergen's diverse cycling routes and convenient bike rental options make it an excellent destination for cyclists. Whether you're looking for a leisurely ride through the city or a challenging journey through the mountains, Bergen has something to offer for every cyclist. Remember to follow traffic rules, wear appropriate safety gear, and enjoy the ride!

9.3 Fjords and Water Activities

Bergen, often referred to as the gateway to the fjords of Norway, is surrounded by some of the most stunning fjords in the world. These natural wonders offer a plethora of water activities for visitors to enjoy. In this section, we'll explore the fjords near Bergen and highlight some of the best water activities available.

Fjords Near Bergen

1. **Hardangerfjord**
    - Distance from Bergen: Approximately 75 km (1.5 hours by car)
    - Description: Hardangerfjord is the second-longest fjord in Norway and is known for its breathtaking scenery, including waterfalls, mountains, and orchards. The fjord is a popular destination for hiking, fishing, and boating.

2. **Sognefjord**
    - Distance from Bergen: Approximately 130 km (2.5 hours by car)

- Description: Sognefjord is the longest and deepest fjord in Norway. The fjord and its surrounding areas offer a variety of activities, from glacier walks to scenic train rides.

3. **Nærøyfjord**

- Distance from Bergen: Approximately 150 km (3 hours by car)
- Description: A branch of the Sognefjord, Nærøyfjord is a UNESCO World Heritage Site known for its narrow and dramatic fjord landscape. The fjord is surrounded by steep mountains and is ideal for kayaking and sightseeing tours.

Water Activities in the Fjords

1. **Fjord Cruises**

- Description: Fjord cruises are one of the most popular ways to experience the beauty of the fjords. There are various cruise options available, ranging from short sightseeing tours to longer day trips that explore multiple fjords.
- Operators: Fjord Tours, Norway in a Nutshell, and Rodne Fjord Cruise are some of the companies that offer fjord cruises from Bergen.

2. **Kayaking**

- Description: Kayaking is an excellent way to get up close and personal with the fjords. Paddle through calm waters and admire the towering cliffs and waterfalls.
- Operators: Njord - Sea Kayak and Wilderness Adventure and Fjord Adventures offer guided kayaking tours in the fjords near Bergen.

3. **Fishing**

- Description: The fjords and surrounding coastal areas are rich in marine life, making them ideal for fishing. You can fish for salmon, trout, and other species.

- Operators: You can join guided fishing tours or rent a boat and equipment from local operators like Bergen Fjord Fishing.

4. **Stand-Up Paddleboarding (SUP)**

- Description: For a more relaxed water activity, try stand-up paddleboarding. It's a great way to enjoy the serene waters of the fjords while getting a workout.
- Operators: Bergen Base Camp and Fjord Expedition offer SUP rentals and tours in the fjords.

5. **RIB Boat Tours**

- Description: For an adrenaline-pumping experience, take a RIB (Rigid Inflatable Boat) tour. These high-speed boat tours are a thrilling way to explore the fjords.
- Operators: Norway Active and Bergen Sea Adventures offer RIB tours that take you through the fjords and along the coastline.

In conclusion, Bergen's proximity to some of Norway's most spectacular fjords makes it an ideal base for exploring these natural wonders. Whether you're interested in cruising through the fjords, kayaking, fishing, or trying out stand-up paddleboarding, there are plenty of water activities to suit all preferences. Always ensure that you follow safety guidelines and check the weather conditions before embarking on any water-based adventures.

9.4 Parks and Green Spaces

Let's begin with **Byparken**, the city park nestled in the heart of Bergen. It's not just a park; it's a cultural canvas where locals and visitors alike gather to enjoy the tranquil pond, watch performances at the music pavilion, and admire the statues that honour Norwegian composers. The park is a stone's throw away from the bustling fish market and Bryggen's colourful waterfront, making it a perfect spot for a leisurely stroll or a picnic with a view.

Next on my list is **Nygårdsparken**, a larger and somewhat wilder park located near the university area. This park is a favourite among students, families, and anyone looking to enjoy a moment of peace under the canopy of mature trees. Its expansive lawns, picturesque ponds, and playgrounds make it an ideal location for leisure and recreation. The diversity of bird species here adds a delightful element of nature watching to your visit.

For those captivated by botanical wonders, the **Bergen Arboretum and Botanical Garden at Milde** is a must-visit. Located about 20 kilometres south of the city centre, this garden boasts a vast collection of both native and exotic plants. The serene pathways winding through the gardens offer a peaceful retreat and an educational journey through the flora of different continents. It's a living museum where every plant tells a story, inviting you to delve into the botanical richness of the world.

Fjellveien, though not a park in the traditional sense, deserves a mention for its green surroundings and breathtaking views of Bergen. This walking path along the mountainside is easily accessible from the city centre and offers panoramic vistas of the urban landscape set against the backdrop of majestic mountains and fjords. It's a favourite among joggers, walkers, and anyone looking to catch a sunset or simply enjoy the fresh mountain air.

Lastly, the **Stoltzekleiven** hike, leading to the top of Sandviksfjellet, offers a green but challenging escape for those looking to test their stamina. This steep trail is lined with lush foliage and provides a rewarding view of the city and beyond from the top. It's a testament to Bergen's unique blend of urban life and nature's bounty, appealing to adventure seekers and nature lovers alike.

Exploring Bergen's parks and green spaces is an essential part of experiencing the city's soul. These verdant havens not only offer a respite from daily life but also showcase the city's commitment to preserving its natural beauty and providing quality outdoor experiences for all. Whether you're meandering through a city park, unwinding in a botanical garden, or trekking along a scenic path, Bergen's green spaces are a testament to the harmonious balance between nature and urban living, inviting you to pause, breathe, and soak in the unparalleled beauty of the Norwegian landscape.

9.5 Adventure Sports and Activities

Bergen, Norway's "City of Rain," is more than just charming cobblestone streets and colourful Bryggen wharf. Nestled amidst dramatic fjords and rugged mountains, Bergen offers a playground for adventure enthusiasts. From scaling dizzying cliffs to kayaking through tranquil waters, this city promises an unforgettable experience for those seeking a thrill.

Hiking Heaven: Bergen's Seven Mountains

Bergen's iconic "Seven Mountains" are a hiker's paradise, offering trails for all skill levels. Whether you're a seasoned trekker or a casual walker, you'll find a path that matches your pace and rewards you with breathtaking vistas.

- **Fløyen and Ulriken:** The most popular choices are Mount Fløyen and Mount Ulriken, easily accessible by the Fløibanen funicular railway or the Ulriken cable car. Both peaks offer panoramic views of the city, fjords, and surrounding islands.

- **Vidden Hike:** For the more adventurous, embark on the Vidden Hike, a scenic 5-hour trek between Mount Ulriken and Mount Fløyen. This moderate-to-challenging trail traverses diverse landscapes, from lush forests to rocky ridges.

Tips:

- Purchase a Bergen City Card for discounted access to public transportation, including the Fløibanen and Ulriken cable car.
- Wear sturdy hiking boots with good ankle support, especially during the winter months.
- Pack layers of clothing as the weather in Bergen can be unpredictable.
- Download a navigation app or consult a map to stay on track.

Kayaking on Calm Waters: Exploring the Fjords

Bergen's picturesque harbour and surrounding fjords provide the perfect setting for a kayaking adventure. Paddle past historical landmarks, traditional fishing villages, and cascading waterfalls, all while soaking in the serene beauty of the Norwegian landscape.

- **Nordnes and Sandviken:** These areas offer sheltered coves and calm waters, ideal for beginners or families. You can rent kayaks from several local companies and join guided tours or explore independently.
- **Hjelte Fjorden:** For a more challenging experience, head to the Hjelte Fjorden, a narrow fjord known for its dramatic scenery and diverse wildlife. This fjord is best suited for experienced kayakers.

Tips:

- Check the weather conditions before heading out, as strong winds and currents can be dangerous.
- Dress appropriately for the water temperature, which can be quite cold even in summer.

- Life jackets are mandatory, and most rental companies will provide them.
- Be aware of your surroundings and respect local maritime regulations.

Beyond the Mountains and Fjords: Adventure Awaits

Bergen offers a variety of other activities for adrenaline seekers.

- **White-water rafting:** Experience the thrill of navigating the rapids of the Raundal River near Voss, just a short train journey from Bergen.
- **Rock climbing:** Bergen boasts several climbing gyms and outdoor climbing crags, catering to all skill levels.
- **Fishing:** Cast your line in the fjords or nearby lakes for a chance to catch cod, salmon, and other fish species.

Remember:

- **Safety first:** Always prioritise your safety and choose activities that match your experience level.
- **Respect the environment:** Be mindful of the natural environment and leave no trace behind.
- **Embrace the local culture:** Engage with local guides and businesses to gain a deeper understanding of the region's unique culture and traditions.

With its stunning scenery, diverse activities, and friendly atmosphere, Bergen is an ideal destination for adventure enthusiasts. So, pack your bags, lace up your hiking boots, and get ready to experience the thrill of adventure in the heart of Norway!

CHAPTER 10

CULTURAL INSIGHTS

10.1 Language and Communication

Bergen, Norway, boasts a vibrant culture and friendly locals. However, navigating communication as a visitor can be helpful, especially if you don't speak Norwegian. Here's a comprehensive guide to the language landscape and essential phrases for your trip:

Official Languages:

- **Norwegian:** The official language of Norway is Bokmål (Bokmål) and Nynorsk (Nynorsk). However, Bokmål is the dominant form used in Bergen and most of Norway.
- **English:** While not an official language, English is widely spoken and understood in Bergen, particularly in tourist areas and among younger generations.

Understanding the Locals:

- **Bergen Dialect:** Be aware that locals might speak a distinct Bergen dialect, which can differ slightly from standard Bokmål in pronunciation and vocabulary. Don't be discouraged if you encounter unfamiliar words or phrases.
- **Non-verbal Communication:** Norwegians are generally known for their reserved nature. However, they are friendly and helpful. Non-verbal cues like a smile and polite gestures can go a long way in communication.

Essential Phrases in Norwegian:

While English might suffice in many situations, learning a few basic Norwegian phrases can enhance your experience and demonstrate respect for the local culture:

- **Hello:** Hei (Hi) / God dag (Good day)
- **Goodbye:** Ha det bra (Have a good one) / Heisann (informal: Bye)
- **Please:** Vennligst (Please)
- **Thank you:** Takk (Thank you) / Tusen takk (Thank you very much)
- **Excuse me:** Unnskyld meg (Excuse me)
- **Do you speak English?:** Snakker du engelsk? (Do you speak English?)
- **I don't understand:** Jeg forstår ikke (I don't understand)
- **How much is this?:** Hvor mye koster dette? (How much does this cost?)
- **Where is...?:** Hvor er...? (Where is...?)

Additional Tips:

- **Carry a Phrasebook:** A small phrasebook can be a handy reference for common phrases and basic vocabulary.
- **Download a Translation App:** Consider downloading a translation app to help with communication in real-time.
- **Be Patient and Respectful:** Remember, locals might not always speak perfect English. Be patient, respectful, and use gestures to aid communication.

Learning a few key phrases and understanding the language landscape in Bergen can go a long way in ensuring a smooth and enjoyable visit for you.

10.2 Customs and Etiquette

Bergen, Norway, welcomes visitors with its breathtaking scenery and friendly locals. However, understanding and respecting local customs and etiquette can significantly enhance your experience and showcase your cultural sensitivity. Here's a guide to navigating social norms in Bergen:

Greetings and Introductions:

- **Handshake:** A firm handshake with direct eye contact and a smile is the standard greeting.
- **Formality:** Norwegians are generally informal, and using first names is common in most situations. However, you can use titles like "Herr" (Mr.) or "Fru" (Mrs.) with surnames in formal settings or when addressing someone older.
- **Personal Space:** Norwegians value personal space. Maintain a comfortable distance during conversations, especially in crowded areas.

Dining Etiquette:

- **Punctuality:** Norwegians are punctual, so arrive on time for invitations and appointments.
- **Invitations:** Invitations are typically verbal, so a simple "takk" (thank you) is a sufficient response to an invitation. Bringing a small gift like flowers or chocolates for the host is a thoughtful gesture.
- **Table Manners:** Norwegians generally follow standard Western table manners. Use utensils appropriately, wait for the host to start eating, and avoid talking with your mouth full.
- **Tipping:** Tipping is not expected in Norway, as service charges are usually included in the bill. However, leaving a small tip if you received exceptional service is acceptable.

Social Interactions:

- **Conversation Topics:** Norwegians are generally reserved, and conversations might not flow as quickly as in other cultures. Avoid overly personal topics and focus on neutral subjects like the weather, local sights, or shared interests.
- **Directness:** Norwegians tend to be direct in their communication, and silence is not considered awkward. However, they are still respectful and polite.

Additional Tips:

- **Dress Code:** Norwegians dress casually, but neatly. Opt for comfortable and practical clothing suitable for the weather, especially if you plan to spend time outdoors.
- **Smoking:** Smoking is prohibited indoors in public places and restaurants. Designated smoking areas are available outdoors.
- **Environmental Friendliness:** Norwegians are passionate about environmental conservation. Be mindful of your waste and recycle whenever possible.

By understanding and respecting these customs and practising basic etiquette, you can ensure a smooth and enjoyable visit to Bergen, fostering positive interactions with the locals and enriching your experience in this beautiful city.

10.3 Religious Sites and Traditions

Bergen, Norway, with its colourful Bryggen wharf and dramatic fjord backdrop, also offers a rich tapestry of religious history and traditions. Exploring these sites and participating in their observances provides visitors with a deeper understanding of the city's cultural fabric and fosters a sense of connection to the local community. Here are 10 recommended religious sites and traditions in Bergen:

1. Bergen Cathedral (Domkirken): Standing tall since the 12th century, Bergen Cathedral is the oldest church in the city and the second-largest cathedral in Norway. Its Gothic architecture and stained-glass windows offer a glimpse into mediaeval craftsmanship. Visitors can attend services, admire the intricate details, and appreciate the peaceful atmosphere within the cathedral walls.

2. Nykirken (New Church): Built in the 18th century, Nykirken, or the New Church, is a prominent landmark in Bergen's city centre. Its distinctive Baroque architecture and spacious interior host regular church services, concerts, and cultural events. Visitors can admire the impressive organ and experience the warm community spirit fostered within the church.

3. The Church of the Cross (Korskirken): Originally built in the 12th century and rebuilt several times after fires, the Church of the Cross holds historical significance. Today, it serves as a vibrant church with regular services and community events. Visitors can appreciate the unique blend of architectural styles and participate in the active community life nurtured by the church.

4. The Salvation Army Citadel (Frelsesarmeens Citadel): The Salvation Army Citadel, established in the late 19th century, is a symbol of social service and community outreach in Bergen. Visitors can learn about the organisation's work in helping the underprivileged and participate in various social events organised by the Citadel.

5. The Mosque and Islamic Cultural Center: Established in the early 2000s, the Mosque and Islamic Cultural Center welcomes Muslims and non-Muslims alike. Visitors can learn about Islam through guided tours, participate in interfaith dialogues, and experience the welcoming atmosphere fostered by the centre.

6. The Buddhist Meditation Center Bergen: Located in the heart of the city, the Buddhist Meditation Center Bergen offers a haven for meditation and mindfulness practices. Visitors can participate in meditation sessions, workshops, and discussions, seeking inner peace and connecting with the principles of Buddhism.

7. The Bergen Quaker Meeting House: The Bergen Quaker Meeting House, established in the late 19th century, provides a space for peaceful reflection and social justice activism. Visitors can learn about Quaker beliefs centred on pacifism and equality, and potentially attend silent meetings, experiencing the practice of contemplative prayer.

8. The Churchyard at Gamlehaugen: The churchyard at Gamlehaugen, the former royal residence, offers a tranquil space for reflection and contemplation. Visitors can wander amidst the gravestones, learn about the lives and legacies of prominent figures buried there, and appreciate the beauty and serenity of the historical cemetery.

9. The Annual Christmas Market: Held in the heart of Bergen during the festive season, the Christmas Market provides a glimpse into Norwegian Christmas traditions. Visitors can explore stalls selling traditional crafts, indulge in delicious holiday treats, and experience the spirit of community and joy surrounding the Christmas celebration.

10. Religious Festivals and Observances: Participating in religious festivals and observances like Easter celebrations, Christmas Eve services, or local faith community events allows visitors to experience the traditions firsthand and gain a deeper understanding of the religious landscape in Bergen.

Exploring these religious sites and engaging with their traditions enrich your visit to Bergen, offering insights into the city's cultural and spiritual tapestry. Remember to be respectful of local practices and dress modestly when visiting religious sites. With an open mind and a spirit of curiosity, you can embark on a meaningful journey of discovery

10.4 Traditional Festivals and Events

A Celebration of Heritage: Exploring Traditional Festivals and Events in Bergen

Nestled amidst the dramatic fjords and vibrant culture of Norway, Bergen pulsates with a unique spirit manifested in its diverse and engaging traditional festivals and events. These celebrations offer a window into the city's rich history, local customs, and vibrant artistic scene, providing visitors with an unforgettable experience.

Embracing the Arts: Bergen International Festival (May/June)

Held annually since 1898, the Bergen International Festival is the largest festival of its kind in Northern Europe. This two-week extravaganza transforms the city into a vibrant hub of music, theatre, dance, and visual arts. International and national artists converge, showcasing their talents in concerts, operas, ballet performances, and exhibitions, captivating audiences with a diverse range of artistic expressions.

Celebrating Music: Nattjazz and Bergenfest (Summer)

Following the Bergen International Festival, music continues to reign supreme with Nattjazz (Night Jazz) and Bergenfest. Nattjazz, a month-long celebration of jazz music, fills the city's nights with the soulful sounds of local and international jazz musicians. Bergenfest, a four-day open-air music festival, takes over the Bergenhus Fortress and surrounding areas, transforming the historic space into a vibrant stage for renowned and emerging artists across various genres.

Honouring the Legacy of Edvard Grieg: Grieg in Bergen (Summer)

Bergen, the birthplace of the celebrated composer Edvard Grieg, pays homage to its musical heritage with Grieg in Bergen. This ten-week festival features a series of concerts held at various locations throughout the city, including the Troldhaugen, Grieg's former home. Renowned artists and ensembles interpret Grieg's iconic works alongside contemporary pieces, offering a captivating exploration of the composer's legacy and influence on the music world.

Embracing Norwegian Culture: Holmenkollen National Costume Day (May 17th)

Bergen joins the nationwide celebration of Norway's Constitution Day, Syttende Mai (May 17th), with its unique local flavour. While official ceremonies and parades are held throughout the city, Holmenkollens National Costume Day stands out. Participants dressed in traditional "bunads," intricately embroidered regional costumes, gather at Mount Fløyen, creating a vibrant tapestry of colours and cultural pride.

A Culinary Adventure: Gladmat (July)

Foodies rejoice at Gladmat, the largest food festival in the Nordic countries. Held annually in the heart of Bergen, this ten-day extravaganza celebrates Norway's culinary scene and the bounty of the region. Local producers, restaurants, and international guests come together, offering a smorgasbord of delicious delights, cooking demonstrations, and workshops. Visitors can embark on a culinary journey, exploring traditional Norwegian dishes, sampling fresh seafood, and discovering innovative food trends.

Beyond the City: The Midsummer Eve Bonfires (June 23rd)

While not exclusive to Bergen, the Midsummer Eve Bonfires hold a special significance in Norwegian culture. Throughout the city, large bonfires are lit on beaches and hillsides, symbolising the burning of winter and the welcoming of summer's long days. This tradition fosters a sense of community as locals gather to sing, dance, and enjoy the festive atmosphere under the midnight sun.

A Celebration of Light: Pepperkakebyen (Gingerbread City) (November/December)

As the nights grow longer and the festive spirit kicks in, Bergen transforms into a winter wonderland with Pepperkakebyen, the Gingerbread City. This charming annual tradition sees local bakeries and individuals come together to create an entire city out of gingerbread houses. The intricate details, whimsical designs, and warm glow of the gingerbread houses create a magical spectacle, attracting visitors from near and far.

These are just a few of the many traditional festivals and events that colour the cultural landscape of Bergen. By participating in these celebrations, visitors gain a deeper understanding of the city's rich heritage, vibrant artistic scene, and enduring traditions. So, immerse yourself in the festivities, savour the flavours, and join the lively spirit that makes Bergen a truly unique and unforgettable destination.

10.5 Historical Context and Modern Life

Bergen, Norway, with its colourful Bryggen wharf and dramatic fjord backdrop, boasts a rich history that has shaped its vibrant modern life. This essay delves into the city's fascinating past, tracing its evolution from a Viking trading hub to a thriving contemporary centre.

Early Beginnings and Viking Legacy (8th-11th Centuries AD):

The story of Bergen begins around the 8th century AD, nestled amidst the picturesque fjords. Initially, a small trading settlement emerged, eventually attracting the attention of Vikings from the west. In the 10th century, King Olav Kyrre, known as "the Peaceful," established Bergen as a permanent trading post, recognizing its strategic location and natural harbour. This marked the birth of Bjørgvin, the Old Norse name for Bergen, meaning "the Mountain Bay."

A Flourishing Trading Hub (12th-15th Centuries AD):

Under King Olav Kyrres rule, Bergen blossomed into a crucial commercial centre. The city secured exclusive rights to trade fish caught in northern Norway, attracting Hanseatic merchants from northern Germany. The Bryggen wharf, a UNESCO World Heritage Site, became the heart of this trade, with its distinctive wooden buildings and narrow alleyways. Bergen also gained prominence as a religious centre, with the construction of Bergen Cathedral, the oldest church in the city.

Challenges and Transformation (16th-19th Centuries AD):

The 16th and 17th centuries brought challenges for Bergen. The Black Death pandemic ravaged the city in the 14th century, and several fires caused significant damage. Despite these setbacks, Bergen remained a significant trading centre. However, the decline of the Hanseatic League and the rise of Oslo eroded Bergen's dominance in the 18th and 19th centuries. Nevertheless, the city continued to be a major port and a centre for shipbuilding and maritime activities.

Modern Bergen: A Thriving City (20th Century and Beyond):

The 20th century ushered in a new era for Bergen. The discovery of oil and gas in the North Sea spurred economic growth, attracting businesses and industries. The city also focused on developing its cultural scene, establishing the University of Bergen, the Bergen International Festival, and several museums. Today, Bergen is a vibrant and cosmopolitan city. It is known as the "Gateway to the Fjords," attracting tourists with its stunning natural beauty, rich history, and cultural offerings.

Modern Life in Bergen:

Modern Bergen offers a unique blend of its historical heritage with modern amenities. Residents enjoy a high quality of life, with access to excellent healthcare, education, and social services. The city boasts a thriving economy, with a strong focus on maritime industries, tourism, and research and development.

Beyond the Tourist Trail:

While Bergen's iconic landmarks and vibrant Bryggen wharf draw visitors, venturing beyond the tourist trail reveals the city's true essence. Exploring the charming neighbourhoods like Nordnes and Sandviken offers a glimpse into local life, with its colourful houses, independent shops, and bustling cafes. Hiking up Mount Fløyen or Ulriken rewards with breathtaking panoramic views, while exploring the fish market allows you to experience the city's vibrant maritime culture firsthand.

Bergen's journey through time reflects resilience, adaptation, and a continuous pursuit of progress. The city's historical legacy is evident in its architecture, traditions, and cultural identity. However, its modern life is equally captivating, showcasing a thriving economy, a commitment to sustainability, and a strong sense of community. Whether you explore its historical sites, delve into its cultural offerings, or simply soak in the beauty of its surroundings, Bergen promises an unforgettable experience.

CHAPTER 11

PRACTICAL INFORMATION

11.1 Currency Exchange and Budgeting

Planning a trip to Bergen, Norway? Navigating currency exchange and budgeting can be crucial for a smooth and enjoyable experience. Here's a comprehensive guide to help you manage your finances:

Currency:

- **Norway uses the Norwegian Krone (NOK).** As of March 5, 2024, the exchange rate is approximately:
    - 1 USD = 10.09 NOK
    - 1 EUR = 11.37 NOK
    - 1 GBP = 11.90 NOK

Exchanging Currency:

- **ATMs:** The easiest and most convenient way to obtain Norwegian Krone is through ATMs. Look for ATMs displaying "Visa," "Mastercard," or "Cirrus" logos to ensure compatibility with your debit or credit card. Be aware of potential withdrawal fees charged by both your bank and the ATM operator.
- **Currency Exchange Bureaus:** While less common, currency exchange bureaus exist at the airport and in the city centre. Rates may vary, so compare before exchanging.
- **Bringing Cash:** Carrying a small amount of Norwegian Krone can be helpful for emergencies or situations where cards aren't accepted. However, it's generally not recommended to bring large amounts due to exchange rate fluctuations and security concerns.

Budgeting:

- **Accommodation:** Costs vary depending on your preferences. Expect to pay anywhere from **500 NOK ($50 USD)** per night for a hostel dorm bed to **2,000 NOK ($200 USD)** or more for a hotel room in the city centre.
- **Food:** Eating out can be expensive in Bergen. Budget **300-500 NOK ($30-$50 USD)** per day for basic meals. Opting for grocery shopping and self-catering can significantly reduce costs.
- **Transportation:** Public transportation in Bergen is efficient and reliable, but can be pricey. Consider purchasing a Bergen Card for discounted access to public transportation, museums, and other attractions.
- **Activities:** Entrance fees for museums and attractions can range from **100-300 NOK ($10-$30 USD)**. Factor in costs for optional activities like hiking tours or boat trips.

Tips:

- **Plan in advance:** Research typical costs for accommodation, food, and activities to create a realistic budget.
- **Utilise travel apps:** Several apps like XE Currency can help you track exchange rates and manage your budget on the go.
- **Look for discounts:** Many restaurants and attractions offer student or senior discounts, so carry appropriate identification.
- **Consider travel cards:** City cards often combine transportation passes with discounts on attractions, offering cost savings.
- **Pack light:** Minimise baggage fees by packing light and utilising public transportation efficiently.

Remember: These are just estimated costs, and your actual spending might vary depending on your travel style and preferences.

11.2 Safety and Emergency Contacts

Ensuring a safe and successful travel experience to Bergen requires more than just an itinerary filled with breathtaking sights and adventurous activities. It's crucial to be aware of safety practices and have essential emergency contacts at your fingertips. Bergen, known for its natural beauty, cultural richness, and historical significance, is a city that welcomes its visitors with open arms. However, like any travel destination, it's important to prepare for the unexpected to ensure your journey is both enjoyable and secure.

Safety in Bergen

Bergen is generally a safe city for tourists, with low crime rates compared to other international cities. However, standard safety precautions should always be observed. When exploring the city, especially in crowded places like the Fish Market or Bryggen, keep an eye on your belongings to guard against pickpocketing. While hiking the surrounding mountains or venturing on fjord tours, wear appropriate gear, be mindful of the weather conditions, and always inform someone about your plans.

In winter, Bergen's streets can become icy and slippery, making falls a common concern. Wearing shoes with good traction or even ice grips can prevent unnecessary accidents. Moreover, when driving outside the city, be prepared for narrow roads and quickly changing weather conditions, especially in mountainous areas.

Emergency Contacts

Having a list of emergency contacts is paramount for dealing with any unforeseen situations. Here are the essential numbers and services you should know:

- Emergency Services: Dial 112 for police, 113 for medical emergencies, and 110 for fire-related emergencies. These numbers can be dialled from any phone, free of charge.
- Medical Assistance: For non-emergency medical assistance, Bergen has several health centres and hospitals. Haukeland University Hospital is the largest in the region, equipped to handle a wide range of medical issues.

- Pharmacies: Pharmacies (apotek) in Bergen can provide over-the-counter medications and first aid supplies. Some pharmacies offer 24-hour service for urgent needs.
- Consulates and Embassies: Knowing the contact information of your country's consulate or embassy can be helpful in case of lost passports or legal issues. Many countries have representatives in Bergen or nearby cities like Oslo.
- Tourist Information: The Bergen Tourist Information Center can assist with general inquiries, lost and found, and provide advice on local services. They are located centrally and can be a valuable resource during your stay.

Safety Tips for Hiking and Outdoor Activities

Bergen's landscape invites outdoor activities, from hiking Mount Fløyen or Ulriken to exploring the fjords. While these activities are generally safe, accidents can happen, particularly with unprepared or inexperienced individuals. Always check the weather forecast before heading out, carry a map and a compass for longer hikes, and have enough food and water. It's also wise to carry a small first aid kit and a fully charged mobile phone. For those planning to hike in remote areas, consider registering your route with a local hiking association or informing your hotel of your plans.

Final Thoughts

Visiting Bergen promises an array of unforgettable experiences, from its scenic beauty to its rich cultural heritage. While the city is welcoming and safe, being prepared for emergencies and understanding local safety advice can make all the difference in ensuring a smooth and enjoyable visit. With the right precautions and awareness, your trip to Bergen can be both adventurous and secure, leaving you free to explore all the wonders this Norwegian gem has to offer.

11.3 Mobile Apps and Online Resources

Planning and Research:

- **Visit Bergen:** https://en.visitbergen.com/ (Official website of Bergen Tourism): This website is your one-stop shop for all things Bergen, including information on attractions, transportation, events, accommodation, and useful tips.
- **Visit Norway:** https://www.visitnorway.com/: The official travel guide to Norway, offering comprehensive information on all regions, including Bergen.
- **Google Maps:** A must-have app for navigating the city, finding points of interest, and planning your itinerary.
- **XE Currency:** Helps you track exchange rates and convert currencies conveniently.
- **Tripadvisor:** Read reviews and recommendations for hotels, restaurants, attractions, and activities in Bergen.

Transportation:

- **VY (Vygruppen):** https://www.vy.no/en (Official website for planning and booking train, bus, and ferry travel in Norway).
- **Skyss:** https://www.skyss.no/en/ (Public transportation provider in Bergen, offering the Bergen Card and real-time travel information).
- **CityMapper:** Provides real-time public transportation information and route planning.

Activities and Attractions:

- **Bergen Card:** https://en.visitbergen.com/bergen-card Offers free public transportation, discounts on attractions and museums, and other benefits.
- **Bergen International Festival:** https://www.fib.no/en/ (Showcases music, theatre, dance, and visual arts during the summer).
- **MTX Connect:** https://mtxc.eu/en/coverage.html (Offers tickets and information for various attractions, museums, and tours).

- **Visit Bergen App:** https://en.visitbergen.com/ (Official app from Bergen Tourism with information on attractions, events, and discounts).

Language and Communication:

- **Google Translate:** Helps translate phrases and text from your language to Norwegian.
- **Memrise:** Offers a language learning app to learn basic Norwegian phrases.

Safety and Security:

- **The Norwegian Police:** https://www.politiet.no/ (Website of the Norwegian Police, English version available).
- **Emergency Services: 112** (Call this number for any emergency, including fire, police, and ambulance).

Additional Resources:

- **The Local Norway:** https://www.thelocal.no/ (Provides news and information about Norway in English).

By utilising these mobile apps and online resources, you can plan your trip to Bergen efficiently, navigate the city easily, and have a safe and enjoyable vacation.

11.4 Local Transportation Tips

Bergen boasts a well-developed public transportation system, making it easy to explore the city without a car. Here are some insider tips to navigate Bergen's transportation network like a local:

Mastering the System:

- **Skyss:** Your go-to resource. Download the Skyss app (https://www.skyss.no/en/tickets-and-prices/buying-tickets/) for real-time schedules, ticket purchases, and route planning. The website (https://www.skyss.no/en/tickets-and-prices/buying-tickets/) also provides valuable information in English.
- **Tickets:** Purchase tickets before boarding buses or trams. Tickets can be bought at kiosks, ticket machines at bus stops and the Bergen Tourist Information Center. Consider a Bergen Card (https://en.visitbergen.com/bergen-card/transport-and-travel) for free public transportation access and discounts on attractions, if it fits your itinerary.

Bus Basics:

- **Network:** Bergen's extensive bus network covers most areas of the city. Look for the distinctive white and red coloured buses.
- **Boarding:** Passengers board through the front door and validate their tickets.
- **Exiting:** Exit through the rear doors unless otherwise indicated.
- **Night buses:** Limited night bus services operate after regular hours.

Tram Tips:

- **Bybanen:** The Bergen Light Rail (Bybanen) offers a convenient way to travel between city centre and suburbs.
- **Frequency:** Trams run frequently, with shorter intervals during peak hours.
- **Accessibility:** Trams are wheelchair-accessible and offer visual and audio announcements of upcoming stops.

Taxis:

- **Availability:** Taxis are readily available at taxi ranks around the city centre, hotels, and popular attractions. You can also hail taxis on the street if the roof light is illuminated.
- **Apps:** Consider using taxi hailing apps like Taxi Norge or Norgestaxi for convenience.

- **Cost:** Taxis are a more expensive option compared to public transportation.

Beyond the City Center:

- **Ferries:** Explore the scenic fjords by taking a ferry from Bergen. Check ferry schedules and routes online or at the Bergen Tourist Information Center.
- **Day Trips:** Plan day trips to nearby towns and villages using a combination of buses and ferries. The Skyss website and app can help you plan your journey.

Additional Tips:

- **Validate tickets:** Always validate your ticket upon boarding buses or trams to avoid fines.
- **Respect fellow passengers:** Be mindful of others and avoid loud talking or eating strong-smelling food on public transportation.
- **Plan your journey:** Utilise the Skyss app or website to plan your route efficiently, especially during peak hours.
- **Consider walking:** Bergen is a walkable city, so explore the city centre on foot whenever possible – it's a great way to soak in the atmosphere.

With a little planning and these local transportation tips, navigating Bergen will be a breeze! Enjoy exploring this beautiful city.

11.5 Visitor Centers and Tourist Assistance

Finding Your Way in Bergen: Visitor Centers and Tourist Assistance

Bergen, with its vibrant history and stunning natural surroundings, welcomes visitors with open arms. To ensure a smooth and enjoyable experience, here's a guide to the city's visitor centres and tourist assistance options:

Bergen Tourist Information Center:

- **Location:** Strandkaien 3, 5013 Bergen (Located near the Fish Market)
- **Website:** https://en.visitbergen.com/
- **Services:**

- Offers information on attractions, events, transportation, accommodation, and activities.
- Sells tickets for attractions, tours, and the Bergen Card.
- Provides currency exchange services.
- Staffed by multilingual personnel to assist visitors with inquiries.

Online Resources:

- **Visit Bergen Website:** https://en.visitbergen.com/
- **Visit Norway Website:** https://www.visitnorway.com/

These websites offer a wealth of information, including:

- Comprehensive listings of attractions, events, and activities.
- Detailed information on transportation options and schedules.
- Interactive maps to help you navigate the city.
- Booking options for hotels, tours, and tickets.

Additional Resources:

- **Bergen Card:** https://en.visitbergen.com/bergen-card
  - Provides free public transportation within Zone 1 (Bergen city centre), free or discounted entry to many attractions, and discounts on other activities.
- **Hotels and Accommodation:** Most hotels and hostels have dedicated staff to assist guests with queries and recommendations.
- **Local Shops and Businesses:** Many shops and businesses in tourist areas have staff who are familiar with the city and can offer helpful information.

Remember:

- Be prepared to ask questions and seek assistance when needed.
- Download the Skyss app (https://www.skyss.no/en/) for real-time public transportation information and route planning.
- Carry a map or utilise online navigation tools to help you find your way around.
- Most locals speak English, so don't hesitate to politely ask for directions or recommendations.

SCAN HERE FOR THE CITY'S GENERAL MAP

I know you might probably t be wondering if I won't add the general city's map, well, please worry less, Freya got you covered, you know your satisfaction is my major concern. Please kindly scan the below QR code or click link **https://shorturl.at/hzT07** to access Bergen's general map. Once you scan the barcode, all you have to do next is to input the name of the location you are heading to. Thank you so much for purchasing my book in the first place, and thanks a million for reading it.

Tell your own Adventure Story Today

My name:

- _____

I travelled along with:

- _____

I arrival experience:

- _____

- _____

- _____

- _____

Where to visit

- _____

- _____

- _____

Where to Eat:

- _____

- _____

- _____

Transit to use:

- _____

- _____

- _____

Where to stay: check-in time and date.

- _____

- _____

- _____

- _____

- _____

- _____

- _____

Outdoor activities to take part in:

- _____
- _____
- _____
- _____
- _____

Personal Drafted Day trips itinerary:

Day 1:

- _____
- _____
- _____

Day 2:

- _____
- _____
- _____

Day 3:

- _____

- _____

- _____

Share your Bergen travel experience:

- _____

- _____

- _____

- _____

- _____

- _____

- _____

- _____

- _____

- _____

- _____

A KIND REQUEST FROM ME

Dear Readers and Travelers,

If this book has been your companion on your journey through Bergen and has enriched your experience, I kindly ask for a moment of your time to leave a 5-star review on Amazon and a nice comment. Your feedback will not only support my work but also help fellow travellers discover the beauty and depth of Bergen through these pages.

I don't take this act of love for granted, and I'm deeply grateful for your support. Sharing your positive experiences and thoughts about this book will ensure that more adventurers can embark on their own Bergen journey with confidence and inspiration.

To leave a review, please visit Amazon.com where you purchased this book.
Your endorsement means the world to me.

Thank you for being a part of this journey, and may your travels continue to be filled with wonder and discovery.

Yours truly,

Prof. Freya Wright.

Printed in Great Britain
by Amazon